Coaching Youth Soccer:

A Complete Guide for Coaches, Players, and Parents

Howie Thompson

COACHES CHOICE

Copyright © 2002 by Coaches Choice Books. All rights reserved.

This book is protected by copyright. No part of this book may be reproduced, stored in a retrieval system, or transmitted in any form or by any means, electronic, mechanical, photocopying, recording, or otherwise, without the prior permission of Coaches Choice Books.

Throughout this book, the masculine shall be deemed to include the feminine and vice versa.

ISBN: 1-58518-658-9
Library of Congress Control Number: 2002104666
Cover design: Jennifer Bokelmann
Book layout: Jeanne Hamilton
Front cover photo: Courtesy of Stephen Dunn/Allsport

Printed in the United States of America

Coaches Choice
P. O. Box 1828
Monterey, CA 93942
www.coacheschoice.com
Fax: (831) 372-6075
Tel: (831) 372-6077

DEDICATION

In my lifetime, I would guess I've coached approximately 2,500 boys and girls. This book is dedicated to each player and each parent, because my coaching experiences helped spawn these words. But, I also owe this book and my deepest thanks to my closest and most loved people in the world. First, my wife, Nancy, who is the only person I have ever met who really understands why I love to coach. She's been my rock through the good times and the bad times. She has always listened to the endless details of each game, and she seems to care what happens. She comes to watch me coach once in a while, and sometimes a parent will ask, "Which child belongs to you?" She always answers, "The big one with the whistle and baseball cap." Next, I want to dedicate this book to my three kids: Jenn, Chris, and Megan. I coached each of them from 5 to 14 years of age. Let me emphasize that it was no walk in the park being the son or daughter of *this* coach. It's hard to be the coach's kid. Thanks for all the memories, and I hope you all had as much fun playing as I had coaching.

Lastly, I want to thank the one person from whom I learned more about soccer than anyone, Whitey Budrekas. Whitey is, arguably, the best skills soccer coach in all of New England. When I first started coaching, my office overlooked a field at the high school where he coached. I watched him every day, watched him teach kids the finer points of the game, picked his brains at tournaments, and I have seen him coach one of the greatest athletes I have ever known, Kristine Lilly. We have been friends for over 25 years now.

I hope you will enjoy this book, and I hope you will gain insight or learn techniques that could help you in the future. If this book helps you with one new drill or to learn one new coaching skill you didn't know, then I will be very happy. My intent was to write a book that would be helpful, informative, a little funny, and always entertaining – kind of like my life.

I had a biology professor in college, a full-blood Cherokee Indian, who once told us, "Learn just one new thing each and every day, and by the time you die, you will have all the knowledge you need." I also liked, "It is always easier to get forgiveness than permission." I've made it a policy to live by these two guidelines for over 50 years now.

I leave you with a poem I wrote about being a coach, which the *National Soccer Coaches of America Journal* published. I wish you all the best. Remember that you could be coaching the next President of the United States some day, so make sure he has your home phone number, just in case he needs advice.

FOREWORD

Coaching Youth Soccer is well written, very accurate and humorous. There is a fine balancing act for the coach of any team between trying to achieve success and pleasing everyone concerned, and there will always be problems, seen and unseen. It is how the right balance is gained between doing the best for the children and for the team.

Winning is not everything. It is how the children progress and learn that is the answer. Yet, the coach can only go on the evidence that is presented to him at training and during the games. The other aspect of the players is seen by their parents, and should have no influence on the coach when it comes to making decisions in relation to matches. Parents can be the most helpful people in the world, but also the most infuriating. But, the coach can have the childrens' undivided attention for a certain part of their day, during which the parents are not allowed to enter, and can teach these children a subject of which the parents have no knowledge or experience. These lessons often closely bond the coach and players together, so that the relationship becomes special and powerful and trusting. It is this trust that is the reward for a coach, and must never be broken.

Well done, Howie. I hope your book is a success. It deserves to be.

Terry Butcher
Assistant Manager
Motherwell FC, Scottish Premier League

TABLE OF CONTENTS

		Pages
Dedication		3
Foreword		4
Chapter 1	Soccer: Roots and Origin	7
Chapter 2	Basic Guidelines for Parents and Coaches	9
Chapter 3	Guidelines for Coaching and Managing Parents	14
Chapter 4	The Organizational Structure of the Team	19
Chapter 5	Age-Specific Coaching Guidelines: 7 to 10 Years Old	21
Chapter 6	Age-Specific Coaching Guidelines: 11 to 14 Years Old	26
Chapter 7	50 Nifty Youth Soccer Drills	32
Afterword		85
About the Author		87

HOW SOCCER BEGAN

God looked around on the seventh day,
And after he rested was heard to say,
"It's a game they need,
One of daring and speed,
A game with a ball
Made for the short and the tall.
One that is fast, where they can throw, kick, and run,
One that can be played in the snow, rain, and sun.
They'll need a field long and wide
And some lines down there to show who's on whose side.
I'll make that ball bouncy, all white and black,
And I'll give them some rules for defense and attack.
There'll be 11 players here and 11 players there,
A goal at each end and some funny uniforms to wear.
I'll keep it quite simple, no hands, just their feet,
And they'll play on a green field where two teams will meet.
They'll learn how to dribble, the ball they will boot,
They'll head, and they'll pass, but most of all shoot.
Now this game I've made, I've created for all,
The young and the old, the short, big, slow, and small.
I think I'll call it SOCCER, just why I haven't a clue,
But I know they will love it, as it's something brand new.
And most of all it's fun as they kick, run, and throw,
And it's something they can keep as they learn and they grow.
So now that I've given a game they can play,
I must go back to resting on this my seventh day.
For the morrow brings a new week and challenges await,
It's Monday morning, and I must turn in the scores before it's too late."

                              Howie Thompson
                              Published in CJSA *NewsLine,* 1990
                              and in the *NSCAA Journal,* 1995s

CHAPTER 1

Soccer: Roots and Origin

Soccer is the world's most popular sport – whether measured by the number of participants or by the number of spectators. It is played by more than 100 million people in over 150 countries. No one really knows when the game of soccer began. Recorded history traces soccer's origins to ancient Greece, Rome, Egypt, and China. Modern soccer began in England, where the first set of rules was published in 1863 by the London Football Association. Soccer has been played in the United States in one form or another for over 100 years, but has only become a major sport since the early 1970s. Depending upon the nation or culture in which the game of Futbol (the Spanish spelling) or Soccer, as we "Yanks" call it, is played, there are various styles of play: Italian style, Brazilian style, Turkish style, and many more.

The first professional soccer league in the United States was founded in 1967. Through the efforts of world-renowned soccer players, such as Pelé and Kyle Rote, Jr., young boys and girls were introduced to this fast-paced game. Children everywhere began playing with the funny looking, round ball that never bounced the same way twice and was quite difficult to control from one player to the next. Aside from the fact that only approximately 10 percent of the nation knew how to instruct youths in the finer points of the game, this was a new sport that kids really enjoyed.

The lords of our most noble bastions of American sports, such as football, baseball, and basketball, expressed contempt for the "new kid on the block" with negative comments like: "It's just a fad." "It will never catch on." "It's too difficult." These, I trust, are the same people who downplayed rock-and-roll and thought the pet rock was a joke.

Two decades later, soccer has not only caught on in the United States, but since 1998, our national men's team has been considered one of the Top 30 teams in the world, and our women's team is the best team in the world today. How did this explosion in popularity happen? How did soccer, a team sport that most American men and women knew very little about before 1970, become the sport with the highest percentage of youth participation in America? One, it's a safe sport to play. There are few serious injuries, especially in comparison with football. Two, the low cost of fielding a soccer team makes it the logical choice for many youth sports organizations. Shorts, shirts, shoes, and a ball are the only equipment needed. And, three, it's fun!

Until 1981, I knew next to nothing or very little about soccer. Over the last 20 years, I have become a student of the game, but more than that, I have observed what I believe is one of the greatest phenomenons of our day – the Americanization of Futbol. Soccer is the new frontier of sports. People, from Carlos the skills instructor to Diane the soccer mom, want to be a part of this fast-growing, opportunistic event happening in America. Many men and women, boys and girls are participating at some level in this sport. Lawyers, doctors, businessmen and women, moms, dads, and even grandparents have caught the wave of this new sports craze.

What does soccer mean? Webster's defines soccer as a form of football played on a field between two teams of 11 players who try to kick a round ball into the opposing team's goal. Some "experts" say that the word is derived from the word "association" that was used in 18th century England because they called the game Association Football. That is really a stretch. Others believe it's because of the long, funny looking sox: hence, sox ball which evolved into soccer. Even a longer stretch. No one could tell me why it's called soccer, but everyone in America knows this game as soccer, and as far as Nike, Umbro, and Adidas are concerned, it doesn't matter.

My definition of soccer is: "A game played on a rectangular field, which is uneven, filled with holes, misaligned, and often located in very remote, hard-to-find places; played by two teams with 11 players each on the field, seven subs who sit on the bench, 30 to 40 screaming adults on the sidelines, two coaches on opposite sides of the field, and three officials who sometimes actually watch the game; played with a round ball that never bounces the same way twice; and played with the objective to put the ball into the opposing team's goal as many times as possible within the allotted amount of time or at least until the screaming parents have lost their voices." Those of us who have attended youth soccer games know this definition very well.

CHAPTER 2

Basic Guidelines for Parents and Coaches

During the fall of their children's eighth or ninth birthday, a group of well-meaning, very enthusiastic parents will approach the local recreation board or soccer board and announce, "We have the makings of a great travel soccer team." Notice the word "great." Not good, not even somewhat talented, but "great." This is problem number one: overexpectations. Even world-famous soccer stars like Kristine Lilly, Tab Ramos, and Pelé were not great at eight years old. I saw Ms. Lilly play at that age. Great? No. She was good.

Why do parents feel the need to pronounce this team of eight-year-olds as "great"? Mainly, because most parents have little or no understanding of what constitutes "good" soccer let alone "great." They, unfortunately, believe this is *the* team to place "small town USA" on the map. That can range from the only team to win a local or regional tournament to the next state champs, to the next Open Cup champs. Ooh ... Open Cup champs! Perhaps, the most coveted title of all youth soccer teams. However, the Open Cup is a national championship for boys and girls age 14 to 23. But, these parents know that with hard work and good coaching, this eight-year-old travel team, which has yet to have its first practice or play a single game will be ready to claim their championship title at 14.

The truth is that this team, composed of approximately 18 eight-year-old players, will have five skills instructors, four head coaches, and roughly 35 different players by the time they are 14 years old. It will not be the same 18 children whose parents are so energetic right now. In fact, only six or seven of the original players will remain together when they start high school at age 14. Why won't these enthusiastic parents stay together and try to keep this group as one? Isn't that the goal everyone agreed to when they were eight? Later in the book, you will find out why. For now, we'll focus on the coach – the cornerstone to a successful team.

Basic Guidelines for Parents

It never ceases to amaze me how parents take an inordinate amount of time to choose the right doctor, dentist, and teacher, but will turn their eight-year-old child over to a man or women they don't know for an equally important part in a child's development – learning sportsmanship and athletics. Time and time again, I have seen parents drop their children off at the first practice without stopping to meet the coach and to learn his or her level of coaching experience and general philosophy for working with children. A checklist for parents who want to make sure their coach is qualified to instruct their children in soccer, or any other sport, is provided in Table 1.

Table 1. Coaches Checklist

- Does he have a resume or a coaching biography? This will tell you where and when he has coached. Check it out. Make sure the information is accurate and truthful.

- Has he coached this particular age and gender and for how long?

- What does the coach feel are his strengths and weaknesses? Be wary if there are no perceived weaknesses cited.

- What is the coach's philosophy on winning and losing?

- What is the coach's three-year goal plan for the team? This is a good question to ask because some volunteer young coaches may be building a resume. You may want him to coach for one, two, or three years, and you should know his intent.

- What is his greatest soccer achievement? If he won the Amsterdam Cup at the age of 15, his goals for an American team may be a bit lofty at first. If he has never won a championship in his life, he may be the perfect coach to take your child to his maximum potential. (*Note:* Not every great coach was a good player.)

- Will he explain to the parents how he would run practice? This way you can get firsthand knowledge of his teaching skills.

- Prior to the initial practice session have the coach sit down with the players in an informal discussion of team rules, practice, format, and his goals.

- Ask how much he expects and wants to be paid. Then tell him how much you are willing to pay. These two figures may or may not be the same.

- Set up a mutually agreed-upon payment system and schedule.

By following this simple checklist, you, as parents, will be able to choose a competent, well-rounded coach, one all the parents have met, seen, and agreed upon – at least for the first season or until he loses three games in a row. After selecting a coach, the next step is to create a Parent Board for the team. The Team Parent Board will be responsible for providing input regarding tournaments, practice schedules, compensation for the coach, and whether the team needs a skills instructor. The skills instructor can and should be the coach if the coach is talented and not just a parent filling the spot. Typically, the skills instructor is also paid, and should meet all of the criteria listed in the Coaches Checklist (see Table 1). The age and talent of the team usually determines whether the skills instructor and coach should or should not be the same individual (see Table 2).

Table 2. Guidelines for Coach/Skills Instructor, or Coach and Skills Instructor

7- to 10-year-olds	Mom or Dad Coach (Volunteer), Skills Instructor (Volunteer/paid)
10- to 12-year-olds Travel	Volunteer Coach, paid Skills Instructor
12- to 14-year-olds Travel	Paid Coach/Skills Instructor
12- to 14-year-olds Premier or Select	Paid Coach, paid Skills Instructors (*Note:* There should be more than one skills person for specific technique training, such as a Keeper Coach.)
14- to 18-year-olds Premier or Select	Paid Coach, several paid Skills Instructors

Volunteerism is fast-becoming a thing of the past in our country and more and more towns and recreation boards are moving to the paid coaches even at the younger ages. Unfortunately, this tends not to be beneficial or necessary, as the younger children need a parental figure on the sidelines, and a disciplined figure for teaching aspects. Volunteers should not feel intimidated by the fact that they may not know the sport, since several high-quality instructional clinics and licensing courses are available in most communities. Many of which are free or will be paid for by the clubs. Boys and girls alike may not want to see their moms and dads screaming instructions from the sidelines, but they do appreciate it when a parent gets involved in their activities. They may never tell you or show you, but most children do love it when their parents help run practice, for example.

Basic Guidelines for Coaches

As the new coach for this group of eight-year-old prodigies, keep your expectations and goals realistic. Remember, you are dealing with eight-year-olds; today's speedy wing may well be next year's fullback. The player with the most skill at eight, or even 10, will often be caught by the true athlete in the group by the time they are 12. Success, whether great or small, should never be measured in wins or losses. Success is often measured in end results, where true success is not the end result, but rather the journey traveled along the way. If everyday you strive to become better than the day before, the wins and loses will take care of themselves.

You want to take baby steps before you run, and you want to have small successes before you win the World Cup. You want to place your team in situations where they can have the opportunity for success. It is also important that they learn to fail. For in failure they will learn to appreciate the true rewards of success. No one, in business, sports or government has ever been a success without first experiencing failure. Perhaps, one of the most glaring examples of this fact is the life of Michael Jordan. Cut from his high school basketball team, he went on to become, arguably, the best basketball player of all-time. Dealing with failure is something you as a coach must learn to handle as well, and effectively managing your own fears will help teach your players invaluable lessons about handling setbacks.

Fortunately, or many times unfortunately, parents will play an integral part of your soccer coaching experience. Monday mornings will hold a whole new meaning as you go off to your "real" job and face five to six phone calls from irate parents one week and calls from parents who want to induct you into the Soccer Hall of Fame the next. Billy Martin, ex-coach of the New York Yankees, once said, "Out of every 10 players on this team, I have three who think I walk on water, three who would just as soon spit at me as look at me, and four who just don't give a damn. The secret is to keep the three who hate me away from the four who don't care." That is the secret to handling parents.

You will notice very early in your career that after a season or two, there will be one group of parents who always tell you how well you're doing, a second group who seldom talk to you except to complain, and a third group who never say anything, just show up, cheer, and say "Hi" and "Bye." This last group is the group you want to encourage to mix and mingle with group number one, your supporters. They are the swing group. If they commingle with the group that supports you, you're in. If they mix and mingle with the other group, you'll suddenly find yourself in the soccer coaches' unemployment line. What I like to do, is use the Parent Board to help mediate situations involving disgruntled parents.

What other pearls of wisdom can I expound on to help make you the most-liked, most-successful, and most-wanted coach? None. You will have to let nature take its course and go with the flow. Let common sense be your guide, listen to the players, not the parents. You will win, eventually, and you will lose. But, you must have and must keep having fun. Having fun should be your number one goal. If you do not make the soccer experience fun, the players will leave to find something else. Today's children have many more choices than we did, and today's athlete is stronger, faster, and more knowledgeable than we were. I do not believe they are as dedicated, but I do believe that they want the discipline and the training, but they also want to know "why." And, you must be prepared to tell them why. Why run laps with a ball and without? Why do push-ups and stretch? Why do cool-downs after a game? Why is a particular drill important? Answer their questions, and they will usually give you maximum effort and their loyalty. Ignore them, and you will be a coach without a team.

CHAPTER 3

Guidelines for Coaching and Managing Parents

Not too far into your coaching career (perhaps as early as the second week), you will find that dealing with the kids is fun, teaching them good sportsmanship is fun, and playing the games and going to tournaments is the most fun. But, one element of youth soccer exists that no matter what state, no matter how good or bad your team, is not fun – the parents. There are basically three types (or stages) of soccer parents, and most, if not all, of the parents go through these stages.

At any given time, you could have one, two, or all three of these types of parents on your team. I cannot give you a sure-fire formula for dealing with these "loving, caring, and always interested-in-fair-play" individuals. One specific, absolute prescription does not exist. However, after nearly 20 years of coaching at various levels, I pride myself on handling individual parents and parent groups in a positive manner that is less detrimental to the overall success of the team. The challenge presented by parents is that you're usually not dealing with rational people; you're dealing with individuals who believe that their young sons or daughters are future Olympians or are scholarship bound for major college programs. If you think I'm exaggerating, let me tell you about the parents of a nine-year-old daughter who asked me if she should concentrate solely on soccer or diversify her talents and play other sports. True story!

This young girl, let's call her Jennifer, was a very talented young athlete who had vision and speed, as well as size for her age. She was able to outrun most of the other team members, had the intuition or perception to know what other players would do, and had the ability to change direction "on a dime." All of this was amazing to those who watched her score goal after goal, until about the age of 11 when the other children in the sport began to grow – and Jennifer did not. She only grew a little more until she was 13. Now, her competitors were as fast if not faster, much bigger, and much more aggressive, as Jennifer was now a bit shy of contact due to her stature. By age 15, Jennifer began to look at other sports like tennis, track, and cross-country, as these were more individual sports, and better suited to her athletic gifts and abilities. Soccer was now her third sport of choice, yet still her love, but she was no longer the "superstar" her parents had once thought she would be. Needless to say, the letters announcing her arrival to the Olympic Training Center and the University of North Carolina were never sent.

Soccer parents can be divided into three different groups: screamers, overachievers, and nonverbals. All three groups come with their own special qualities and characteristics, and each group can both undermine and/or destroy a coach's hard work and efforts if not identified and handled properly.

- *Screamers:* This type of parent can be easily identified, both moms and dads. They will be the ones you can hear from the other side of the field. They begin screaming with the opening kickoff, stop around half time, begin again with the second half kickoff, and are out of voice (and breath, thank God), by the end of the game. "Let's go out there," "Defense," "Kick the ball," "Be aggressive," "Hustle," and "Don't just stand there, do something," are a few of the more tame phrases heard from this motley crew. You also hear: "Hey, ref, are you blind?" "Is your kid on the other team, ref?" "What do they have to do, draw blood?" "You stink!"

    This is where you and the team manager must step in to calm this person down for two reasons: One, and the most important, you are teaching sportsmanship to your young, impressionable players, and, second, the referee or official working the game will not tolerate very much of this behavior before removing you as the coach or stopping the game, neither of which is good for the players to experience. What do you do with these "lovely" parents? Review what is acceptable sideline parental behavior, and remind them of the old kindergarten axiom, "If you don't have something nice to say, then don't say anything at all." What has worked well for me is to get the team manager to start a system of yellow and red cards (given out by a designated parent at each game). A yellow card is a warning, and a red card is notice to leave the field until they can regain composure. This is done in an attitude of good, clean fun, while sending out the clear message that this type of behavior is completely unacceptable and will not be tolerated. I've been amazed at how well this system works. It's remarkable how quickly "screamers" can gain control after they've been "carded."

- *Overachievers:* This group of parents are "classics" in youth sports. It's the tennis mom, the baseball dad, and, of course, the soccer mom and dad. These parents all believe they have the next superstar, like the outstanding soccer player from their community who went on to greatness.

    Fortunately, in our community we had Kristine Lilly, probably the best midfielder on the USA Women's National Team and Gold Medal Olympian, winner of the first Women's World Cup, and that rarest of commodities – a modest superstar. Kristine was truly a wonderful athlete from the time she was five years old and, to this day, is the nicest young woman I have ever had the pleasure of knowing (besides my wife, Nancy). On each team, we have always had parents who were absolutely positive they had the next Kristine, but their child either did not live up to the hype or quit the sport due to undue pressure. These parents will do everything and anything they can to help you, which can be perceived as preferential treatment by the other parents. However, because of their enthusiasm to have the "best" for their child, these parents often make a wonderful addition to the Parent Board. They will find tournaments to play, handle the setup of scrimmages, find the best hotels to stay at while traveling, and will purchase the best uniforms for the kids. But, as the coach, always remember to maintain (and use, if necessary) your veto power, so this group of parents do not begin to "run" the team in your absence. A well-oiled machine runs well because the oil gets to all the parts and not just the main group of pistons.

- *Nonverbal:* This is the most dangerous group of parents you will encounter, because unlike the other two types who let you know what they want, this group just quietly watches, takes notes, says very little, and acknowledges even less. They will always be the first ones at the parent meetings and the first ones to leave. Most of the time, they keep to themselves on the sidelines and don't linger to discuss the game with you or other parents. When they do speak, it is usually in time of crisis or tension, and they will be the parents that the rest of the group will listen to. They will either praise you or bury you, and they will be thought of as the parents who are the most knowledgeable. To get this group on your side, you will need to work hard to gain their trust. They should be put in charge of the team budget or given the task of finding the proper "skills" person. They should be on your team Parent Board, so that this Board has credibility. This parent group is participating in this particular activity because their child likes it. The minute their child dislikes any part of it, they and their child are likely to be gone, usually without notice or fanfare.

Don't get me wrong. Parents are the backbone of youth sports teams and can be a wonderful addition to a successful organization, if you know how to properly handle them. As previously stated, no magic phrases or mystical ways exist for handling a parent group. Rather, plain common sense, followed by logic and a cool head, is the key ingredient for effectively working with your team's parents.

Confrontation is typically not a good alternative for handling problems and should always be used as a last resort. Divide and conquer has always worked for me. Never get into a heated discussion with a group unless you have already stacked the deck before the meeting. One on one is a much more advantageous way of handling most parent problems. Always schedule the meeting after a practice or on an off day – never before or during practice, or before or after a game. Such a meeting will take your attention away from the players, which is not fair to them. If you explain this philosophy up front at your first parents' meeting, you will have very few problems. This brings me to my next topic regarding parents, and that is the parent meeting.

The parent meeting is a wonderful opportunity for you and your staff to discuss the workings of the team, the goals of the team, and what you intend to do with this particular young group of athletes. The meeting should last a maximum of one to two hours. Have your manager send the agenda out before the meeting, and stick to the agenda, allowing little or no time for idle "chitchat." This will move the meeting along, allow enough time to cover what's important, and set the tone for future meetings. Having short, productive meetings will encourage strong, parental participation in future meetings. If possible, have someone other than yourself, such as the team manager, president, treasurer, or a designated parent, run the meeting. Be sure to meet with this person beforehand to help ensure that all goes smoothly.

A typical agenda might look like the following:

- Welcome - Team Manager
- Budget or treasurer's report - Team Finance person
- Practice times, days, and locations - Team Manager
- Team philosophy - Coach (expectations, playing time, practice habits, etc.)
- Tournaments - Team Manager
- Team Structure - Team Manager and Coach
- Questions
- Wrap-up (coffee and snacks optional)

Having an agenda allows for the business-related items, such as the budget, practices, and team philosophy, to be discussed early, so that other items, like tournaments, team structure, and the ever-popular open-question time, can be held to the end when everyone is eager to leave. Having coffee and snacks at the end will also move the meeting along and give parents a chance to talk among themselves. However, be careful not to let too much mingling occur, because as Billy Martin once said when asked what was so hard about managing the Yankees, "Well, you know, when you have 10 guys sitting on the bench, you're always gonna have three guys who hate you, three guys who love you, and four that just don't give a damn. The hardest thing is to keep those three that hate you away from the four that don't give a damn." It would be wise to remember this quote anytime you see three or more parents talking intensely together. I leave you with this little ditty on parents.

The Parents' Ditty

Parents come in all shapes and sizes.
They scream, they yell, and sometimes they complain.
They bring their kids to games and practices
In the cold, the sun, and even the rain.
Their child is perfect; they never do wrong.
It's always the other parent's child who just doesn't belong.
They want to know why their child isn't playing
As much time as Jimmy or Matt or even Lila or Sue.
It doesn't much matter just how much talent they have,
They want to know right now just what you're gonna do.
They're never quite happy with what you have to say,
And they'll always ask another parent what they think is right.
They'll call the team manager and the League President, too.
And, then they'll call you, always very late at night.
A good parent has vision, though sometimes myopic
And sees only the good things their child has to do.
The rest of the team, well that's for the Coach to handle.
And, you know who the Coach is ... that's you.

                                        Howie Thompson

CHAPTER 4

The Organizational Structure of the Team

After tryouts but before the first practice, you will need to develop the team structure or organization. First and foremost, you must have a team manager, whose job it is to oversee everything. This position is responsible for all the administrative duties, so all you have to do is coach. With the team manager's assistance, you will need to identify at least three volunteer parents to make up the Parent Board. The Parent Board, the coach, and the team manager should function as an efficiently working Board of Directors which can defuse problems, handle policy issues, and determine the philosophy of the team. The Board of Directors should be created similar to an organization with a president, vice president, and treasurer.

Depending on the team, either Travel or Premier (e.g., Select, ODP, All-Star), the structure will take on slightly different looks. For a Travel team, made up of primarily "in-town" players, your Board is easily picked by you and the team manager from those parents who have showed the most interest and involvement. For the Premier group, this now becomes a little more political because you want to have a good mix of people who are interested, people who are knowledgeable, and people who really want to work. This, coupled with the fact that you also want to assign jobs and responsibilities so that no one town or region can dominate, makes this task a bit more difficult. Whatever the team, the jobs and their requirements are very similar and look something like the following:

- *President:* Ideally, this is the politically correct individual who acts as the spokesperson for the team. He will attend, with the team manager, all town meetings related to the team, and, for the most part, run the parents' meetings. Truly a figure head in a "Queen of England" sense of the word. This person's only power is that as president he can sign checks if the treasurer is not available.

- *Vice President:* This person handles the parent problems, coaching problems, field problems, and, in general, must be very knowledgeable about the rules and regulations of soccer. This would be a great job for the parent we previously talked about who "knows everything." This person should also be very organized since he coordinates all the details of traveling to tournaments, such as reservations for hotels, restaurants, etc.

- *Treasurer:* Every team has a mom or dad with capabilities or experience in a finance-related field. This should, ideally, be that person's job. The treasurer sets up bank accounts, pays the bills, reconciles the accounts, and gives the budget reports at the parents' meetings. With the coach and the team manager, they draft the original budget based on income versus expenses.

- *Team Manager:* There isn't enough room in this book to list everything a good team manager does. He sets up tryouts, distributes roster forms at tryouts, collects forms after tryouts, follows up with parents who don't turn in these forms; types, retypes, and then changes the team roster to be sent to the state, making sure all dates and names are correct; creates and then recreates all passes to be approved by the state association, then picks them up, puts them in alphabetical order on a ring, and holds on to them for safekeeping; has all medical release forms signed, dated, and notarized for tournament play, lines up all the tournaments for approval by the Board; sets up all home and away games with other managers; distributes a weekly newsletter that lets the parents and team players know everything that was discussed at previous parents' meetings; regularly contacts the coach; makes sure the skills instructors show up on time; and makes sure every player receives a birthday card on their birthday. After all this – and more, he gets a lousy T-shirt that says, "I am the Proud Parent of #7 and Team Manager." I have been extremely fortunate to have some wonderful team managers over the years. They have allowed me to do the thing that I love and do best ... coach!

- *Coach:* As a board member, it is your job to evaluate talent each season, set up and operate an adequate practice schedule, and coach the team fairly to the best of your ability. Each season you should hand out a written evaluation of each child's performance noting their strengths and weaknesses. This type of evaluation comes in handy at the tryouts each year when you have to "cut" a child and replace him with another. If you do this arbitrarily with no notice, you are asking for problems. If, however, the parent has seen in writing the child's shortcomings, little or no discussion occurs. Always be honest, and always be fair. Remember that you will often hear things from these children that they would never tell their parents. You will have a unique relationship with them. You can be their friend, but they have to know where the line is drawn. They – and you – cannot cross it. It has been for me, and it can be for you the most rewarding time of your life, but at times the most frustrating. Those of us who love coaching know all too well the ups and downs; but, we would have it no other way.

The most important contributing factor to building a team is to have competent, willing parents to serve as leaders. The most successful teams I have coached were those teams that had 12 to 14 parents of the 18 players involved somehow with the team. And, I always followed Billy Martin's advice to keep the three who hated me away from the rest. We used to put them in charge of securing the nets to the goals. We would get them so tired before the games they didn't have much to say.

CHAPTER 5

Age-Specific Coaching Guidelines: 7 to 10 Years Old

Over the years, I have coached U-5 to U-19 – boys and girls. The 7- to 10-year-olds are by far the most fun age group to work with. Why? Because like an artist you are working with a clean canvas, and you can create your own masterpiece. Parents' expectations are still within reason, and the officiating is lax enough that the players can still learn without fear of failure. Fun is the key word here. The more fun the greater the success. If only this would still hold true later, for these same players.

Between the ages of 7 and 10, boys and girls can, and often do, play on the same team versus each other, an all girls team or an all boys team. It really doesn't matter. The key factor for this age group is skill. Skill development and fun should go hand in hand for this age group. It's amazing how much can be learned in a user-friendly atmosphere where the players don't even realize they are learning. Skill development for this age group should consist of the following techniques:

- Trapping
- Ball control
- Dribbling with small touches
- Throw-ins
- Controlling a rolling ball
- Playing a dead ball
- Understanding the game

Basic Guidelines for Coaching and Instructing 7- and 8-year-olds

You will notice that "kicking the ball properly" is not on the list. I've seen many coaches spend hours trying to teach 8-year-olds the proper way to pass, only to have them kick it with their toe in a game. And, you know that's exactly what they will do 90 percent of the time, so why bother. Camps, well-intentioned friends, and clinicians will spend days, weeks, and months taking inordinate amounts of the parents' money to teach little Johnny or Sally the proper technique for kicking a soccer ball. I have always been under the impression that if the ball goes where the player wants, it ultimately goes into the net. How it got there does not matter at this age. So, don't waste your time when there is so much more to teach these young players.

The first skill I listed above is trapping, and rightfully so, for if a player learns to trap a ball successfully and keep it at their feet, they will be truly successful as they progress to higher levels of play. Teaching young players at this age to trap a ball is similar in technique to controlling a greased watermelon in the water. A successful trap in soccer is one that stays close (less than three yards away) and allows the player to keep control. A good analogy is telling the players to "catch the ball with their feet," thereby creating a helpful image in their minds. Always remind them to trap with whichever foot is coming away from the ball and not toward it so a "soft foot" is created.

Ball control goes hand in hand with trapping as it's the next step in moving the ball where it should go. Ball control drills are as plentiful as there are coaches. However, I have always been in favor of the "small touch" drills that allow players to touch the ball every step while keeping their heads up and not looking at the ball. These drills should be approximately 15 to 20 minutes in length, and should consist of two to three different drills, moving a group of 20 players through several stations.

Throw-ins are something I have taught to the youngest players because I have always felt that this is a skill easily taught and learned and one that can change the advantage of a youth soccer game. If you teach your players the proper way to throw a ball in, they can take control of a dead ball situation and quickly put your team on offense, while the other team just watches. Teaching throw-ins is like teaching a pitcher to throw a baseball or a quarterback to throw a football properly. You start from the ground up and build to a standing throw. Take the time to help each player develop this skill, as it will pay great rewards during game time. This is a 15-minute drill utilizing all the players and one ball for two players at a time.

One of the funniest things in life is watching a 7-year-old boy or girl try to catch and control a rolling ball and stop it. Several things can happen when a very young player attempts this, and, unfortunately, most of them are not good. They can trip over the ball; they can run right past the ball – never touching it; they can get up to the ball and continue to kick it in the wrong direction; they can run and run and run, never catching the ball, and then fall exhausted to the ground as the ball rolls out of bounds; or they can actually catch and control the ball. At which point, they now have to decide what to do with it. The drill here is actually quite simple. Break up the group into pairs, have one player roll a ball away from his partner, and have the other one chase it down. Give the instruction to simply catch the ball and stand on it with one foot.

Dead balls are those times in a game when the ball actually stops and is played from a "restart" position. There are several of these moments during the game. Knowing what to do, and how to use these "time-outs" to your advantage will make you the wonderful coach I know you want to be. Dead balls occur when the ball rolls out of bounds, a foul occurs, or when a goal is made. These dead balls are called one of the following: Corner Kick, Penalty Kick, Direct Kick, Indirect Kick, Goal Kick, and Kickoff. The word Kick is used in every instance. That would mean that a restart of the game must happen with a foot striking the ball. This is where most parents love to voice their opinions loud enough so that not only the players can hear, but also anyone walking within two miles will know exactly what they want. Such pearls of wisdom as, "Kick it," "Kick it hard," "Send it long," "Send it low," "Chip it," "Long ball," "Step up," and my personal favorite, "Punt it." (I actually heard this last one in a U-12 Premier Game from a center forward's dad.) Dead ball drills vary, but repetition is the key, again utilizing all the players, two players as partners with one ball.

You now have 45 minutes to an hour of skill work for your young group to practice each and every session. You are ready to teach them the concepts needed for understanding the game. At ages 7 to 9, the understanding of the game focuses on the most basic of game strategies (e.g., we are here, and our goal is there). We don't want the other team to go here (showing your net), and we want our team to go here (showing the other teams net). This sounds like tongue in cheek, but truly this is an important part of the game to get these young players to understand. Teaching your charges to go from here to there in the most expedient manner – with the ball – will make your coaching career a dream, and hold you in the highest esteem with the one group that can make your life a living hell – the parents.

Basic Guidelines for Coaching and Instructing 9- and 10-Year-Olds

Now that you have taught your young boys and girls the basics, the next age group is one filled with learning, optimism, and fun. The 9- and 10-year-old athlete can range from one who has great vision, tremendous athletic ability, and a keen sense of the game to one who can't tie his shoes without pulling a muscle. All of what you have taught your 7- and 8-year-olds, must now be retaught to this group and augmented so they don't feel like it has become repetitive and boring. The drills can last longer, and you must keep the entire group involved in what is perceived as a unified skill session, because some of these young players have already been to the U.S. Mega Camp of Futbol where they have learned things you have never seen. They have learned the "Maradona," they have been taught how to "mark" as a defender, have picked up buzz words like diagonal runs and takeovers, and now they know that the center striker is the best position.

Not to worry, that is why you have purchased this book. What you need to do now is become creative, and vary the drills and skills so the group thinks there is something new everyday. Along with the above drills, it is now time to introduce some new and exciting skills and drills for the 9- and 10-year-old players.

Trapping is still the primary skill and, believe it or not, will remain so well into their high school careers. But, now you must encourage the players to "trap and look." This is a term that, when used, will make you seem like you took the summer to train with Brazil. Trap and look simply is the same trapping skill as above, but now we teach the players to raise their heads to find an open space, a teammate, or the goal.

Learning to strike a ball properly is a term that most of your players have heard at camp or from some other soccer expert. It is a skill that needs to be worked on at every practice. Couple this with a shooting drill, and you now have incorporated goalkeeper training in your session. The parents and players are now looking at you as if they have found the "Pelé" of coaching. Enjoy this lofty position, as it is often short-lived.

Heading the ball is now introduced as a means of gaining an advantage. Couple this with throwing and/or long balls/dead balls, or punting practice from the keeper, and you now have a training session to rival the best high school program.

Teaching the tactics of the game now becomes more involved because you want to instruct the players in the "offside" rules, playing with and without the ball, incorporating diagonal runs and takeovers into game play, corner kick drills, goal kick plays, and other dead ball plays. Defense becomes the word of the day, as the 10 to 7 and 13 to 12 game scores now become 3 to 0 or 1 to 1 low-scoring contests, and it becomes more important for your players to learn how to play defense. "Goal side, ball side" becomes a phrase you use everyday. Teaching technique rather than results begins to become increasingly important. While most of your teams will be playing small-sided soccer, 7 v 7, some of the country still want to put these small 9-

and 10-year-old bodies on a big field where they do not learn how to reach the goal from a corner nor do they know how to get the ball out of the box. It has always amazed me, that in America, we begin our basketball and baseball players on small surfaces to achieve greater success at an early age, yet when it comes to soccer, we want to put them on a big field. Why? Because the big people, parents, have no idea how to teach this game and are frustrated when they think a smaller field means smaller results. Remember in soccer (as in most of life) size does not matter.

The 9- and 10-year-old group will have one more change and that is the gender of your team will now be one. Most states mandate this, except for the occasional young girl whose parents think she can be challenged by playing with the boys. This fact is largely a matter for debate. However, I have never heard of a boy not being allowed to play up when he had the talent to do so. Therefore, why should we not allow a girl to play at whatever level she can succeed. That's the key word here, succeed. Success is many things to many people, but to a 10-year-old girl, it may be as simple as making a boys' team, then choosing to play with her friends. Just let 'em play!

Certainly, as a first-time experience with this great sport and this age group, the 7- to 10-year-old athletes can be fun, frustrating, and truly the most exciting time of their – and your – life. You might be the very first coach a child has and he may remember something you say or do forever. Keep in mind that you have the responsibility of teaching these young players sportsmanship, as well as the skills of soccer. They will often mimic your actions, both good and bad, off the field. Be a coach and all that goes with that title. Be a friend, a parent, a confidant, and a teacher. Be tough, but be fair, and have rules that everyone must adhere to. Be honest (kids can always spot a phony), and remember to treat every player as if he were your own child. If your son or daughter is on the team, have an assistant coach them and evaluate their talent to avoid charges of nepotism (don't be surprised if such accusations are leveled anyway). Always evaluate each player, in writing to the parents, at the end of the season. In closing, I'd like to pass along a tip I picked up several years ago, and I have used it with great success. Always remember that this is a game and not real life. Have fun, have fun, and then when you think the team is ready, have even more fun. Enjoy!

CHAPTER 6

Age-Specific Coaching Guidelines: 11 to 14 Years Old

The ages of 11 to 14 can be some of the most exciting times of a young boy's or girl's life, as they begin to transition from childhood to young adulthood, move from Elementary School to Middle School or Junior High, and discover that they are now bigger, stronger, faster, and better at most of the things they try – especially athletics. It can, however, also be one of the most challenging times of their lives because they are going through significant physical and emotional changes. (In your best Rod Serling voice, "You have entered the Puberty Zone.") Make no mistake. At times you will feel like you're caught in the Twilight Zone when you try to coach this age group. You'll want to pull your hair out (whatever is left) trying to keep this group focused on the tasks ahead. Two totally separate and distinct development levels exist: 11- and 12-year-olds, and 13- and 14-year-olds. Each group presents a unique set of circumstances and challenges.

Basic Guidelines for Coaching and Instructing 11- and 12-Year-Olds

The 11- and 12-year-old soccer players have now grown up, or so they think. The playing field has increased to regulation size, the number of players has changed from 7 to 11, and, for the next two years, the size of the ball has gone from a size three (in most states) to a size four. In addition, the players (both boys and girls) begin to experience physiological changes that effect athletic performance. For example, boys start to develop greater muscle mass, strength, and power, while girls begin or soon will begin menstruation. The male athletes are now able to use their muscles in ways they could not before. They may also have great difficulty controlling their new found level of strength, oftentimes sending passes way out-of-bounds and shots, which would normally be deftly accurate, into the next zip code. The female athletes, on the other hand, struggle with their newfound "friend," PMS, and may experience significant mood swings that can run the gamut of emotions.

Like the males, young women can experience significant improvements in muscle strength and power in response to resistance training.

As stated at the beginning of this chapter, coaching 11- and 12-year-olds can be a most challenging and frustrating time for coaches and players. It can also, however, be among the most rewarding experiences. It has been my personal experience that coaching this age group allows me to teach more tactics, greater skills and techniques, and actually have a game plan other than kick and run.

For this age group as with the 7- to 10-year-olds, trapping heads the list of skill development. This is the ideal age for introducing the "body trap." As with all drills, repetition and repeated practice are critical for ensuring that your players hone this skill. Trapping the ball with the chest and bringing it to the feet is essential for being able to control the mid-level pass or the 50/50 ball."

Tactically, you can now begin to teach your players the importance of a diagonal run and the value of keeping the ball close for control. Teaching the takeover and introducing this age group to corner kick plays and dead ball plays is not only fun, but keeps them advancing on the learning curve.

Perhaps, the most enjoyable trait of this age level (from a coach's perspective) is their enthusiasm and how quickly they learn. The 11- and 12-year-olds are like sponges waiting to soak up information like droplets of water on a kitchen sink. And, like the sponge that sometimes soaks up the spilled spaghetti stain as well, they can easily be marred by negative behavior. Good habits are hard learned, and bad habits, like toe kicking, are harder to remove. Patience and tolerance become virtues that can help you attain sainthood.

An arguably more difficult challenge is managing the expectations of your players' parents. Around age 11 or 12, the parents who have had visions of the World Cup for their little Jane or Johnny, unfortunately, become more aggressive and demanding. Your only salvation comes when you see your group of talented young soccer players take the ball on their own 18-yard line, make two outstanding touch passes to move the ball out, then your left midfielder makes a diagonal run from the centerline to the opposing 18-yard line, outdistancing three defenders on the way. At the 18-yard line, this wonderful young player now performs a perfect stop dribble, turns the ball back, and crosses it with deft precision to the left wing who is making a run at precisely the right moment. The left wing traps the ball at his feet, keeping the required 3-foot distance away, takes one dribble then sends what appears to be an accurate shot on goal to the far post. Out of nowhere comes your left wing, lays out flat in the air, and drills the ball into the back of the net like a bullet shot from a gun. GOOOOOOOAAAAAAALLLLLLL!

This all happened within a two-minute span of time, but it unfolded in front of you as if in slow motion. This is as good as it gets! After the 1-0 win, your parents and players laud your performance as a coach, and attribute the fine play to your talents and expertise. As you walk off, equipment in tow, a small voice behind you calls, "Coach Jones." You turn to see one of your players, the one who is considered #18 out of 18 players running toward you with a smile, eyes wide with glee, and every muscle in his body announcing joy. "Thanks, Coach. Thanks for putting me in the last 10 minutes to play. I know the parents didn't want me to play. If you didn't have faith in me, I never could have put my head on the ball and scored that goal. I just wanted to let you know how much it meant to me that you had faith in me." As he gives you a high five and turns to walk away, you pick up your bags of balls, throw them over your shoulder, adjust your sunglasses, and wipe a tear off your cheek. Now you know why you do it, now you understand what it's all about. It's not the wins or the losses nor the parents who want to be bosses, it's about the players, it's about loving competition and teaching your players to love it, and it's about how much fun and rewarding coaching can be. At the end of the day, you can hold your head up high as you pack up your things to go home. You know in your heart you do this for the right and most admirable reason – you do it for all the girls and boys.

Basic Guidelines for Coaching and Instructing 13- and 14-Year-Olds

The difference, the main difference, with both boys and girls aged 12 to 13 is "the opposite sex." At 12, it was yucky to be seen with a member of the other gender. Now at 13 and certainly by 14, in many circles you may be considered weird if you're not already dating or at least have shown an interest in the opposite sex. This can be a wonderful, outstanding, and sometimes frustrating age to coach. Some coaches even get to the point where they say, "Okay, I'm done. Let's find a 'professional' to handle this group." I find the 13- and 14-year-olds the most enjoyable to coach. Not only do they experience vast and rapid hormonal changes, they also experience rapid improvements in their ability to think, react, and achieve. The word "why," which will become your most hated word, precedes everything this age group does. "Okay" will be the other word you will learn to hate, as it becomes the answer to every question you have. "How was that drill?" "Okay." "How do you like playing defense?" "It's okay." "How would you like to run three miles for every time you say okay?" That always gets a different response, usually "why"? Boys' versus girls' games now become futile at best, as the girls don't want to show up the boys and the boys are amazed at how good the girls look in shorts and tank tops.

Tactical and technical work now becomes very important, whether you are dealing with the U-13/14 Premier player or the Rec/Club player. Your goal as coach is to get these players ready for high school play, if that is where they are headed. By now, most of the players you had when they were 9 or 10 have either gotten more serious about the game or have gone to alternative sports like baseball, football, field hockey, track, swimming, and hockey. Repetition and variation should become part of each training session, with a large amount of time set aside for game play and controlled scrimmage. Controlled scrimmage, as opposed to scrimmage, is where the coach is on the field as a referee/coach. You will stop the game several times throughout each half, noting tactical and technical advantages and disadvantages. The players hate this, but it is one of the best teaching tools a coach can use – actual game play that can be stopped, positively reinforced, and continued. It's also an excellent way to work on game conditions, corner kicks, dead balls, and penalty kicks. Ideally, controlled scrimmaging should be done every week, sometimes two times a week, depending on whether it's a youth team or a high school team.

By this age, the Premier or Select group in your town will have "stolen" the "best" players from your team, leaving only those interested in playing travel or club soccer. Depending on the area or region, several towns may have to combine teams to keep the less talented players intact together, while the most talented go on to "the next level." This is the phrase that you will hear now day in and day out, because the parents are always concerned about the "next level." I always found it interesting that when asked what that meant, not a single parent could explain.

However, let's talk about the "next level," because at this age you will hear this phrase a lot. Every parent wants to know what the next level is for this team or the other team. In fact, I was fired from a U-14 girls' team because I told the parents that (1) the level of the team was right where they should be, and (2) the next level for most of them was high school. This was a team of young girls that I had coached since they were 11 years old, and some of them since they were five. We were a good team, (98-23-18 over two years) and at times a great team, achieving wonderful results. But, sometimes we were not so great, and sometimes we were downright awful. After a wonderful U-12 year where we got to the finals of our State Cup, won several major out-of-state tourneys, and even won a Gold Medal in two consecutive State Olympic Games, we began to slump. We opened our U-13 Spring Season with five loses in a row, giving up more goals in five games than we had in three seasons prior. The parents got together and fired the skill instructor, sighting that he was too tough and the girls did not like him. The fact was that he was the best skill instructor in our region, and, yes, he was tough, but he, like the three skill instructors prior to him, had the same opinion – nice team, nice girls, poor work ethic. Two more losses and a tie in a tourney, and now the parents were looking for my head as well. I met with the manager and was told that "all of the parents" felt a change was needed. I asked to speak to the girls to let them know I would be leaving, as I had handpicked each girl for this team. The concept was that I would leave at the end of the season (some six games to go). After our meeting, the girls went out and beat a close rival team 1-0 in a great game. The very next Monday, I was fired by fax – no face-to-face meeting, no reasons, just several of the parents getting together and making this decision for the group.

Remember what I said about keeping the three parents who hate you away from the rest? This was a classic example of why that is an important guideline to follow. Three or four parents had spoken via phone to three or four others, and they made the decision to let me go. When everything came out into the open, the girls were not happy, and several parents contacted me, saying, "I didn't want this to happen, but they said it was best or we would lose some players." Soccer politics can be deadly. Parents can get it into their heads that a situation has gone bad, and, within two weeks, things can go from bad to worse. The higher the level of play, the greater the chance that this type of situation will happen. I know of two other cases in our state where coaches were fired with no reason or forethought, just because a few parents thought someone else would be better. Most of the time, these decisions are based only upon the wants and needs of a few individuals. And, when and/or if the right situation appears for these individuals to leave and go elsewhere, they are gone with little or no loyalty to the team or any other players.

Premier often does not mean the best. In most states, the "Premier" concept operates as Select, Level 1, or Tourney Teams. These are teams that have gotten together for a specific purpose, attracting players with greater talents to a program that will introduce them to a higher level of play. However, more often than not, it becomes a bidding war (usually somewhere between $1,000 to $2,500) to get players into a program. The contracted commitment for most players is year round, no participation in other sports or activities is permitted, and the competition for these teams can be fierce. I have seen 12-year-old girls break down in tears because they got cut on the field from the "A" Premier team. I have seen coaches and skills instructors paid $3,000 to $20,000 for a year's work, and I have seen budgets that come close to those needed to run small businesses used to operate these teams. It does not take a math wizard to figure out that this level of soccer is *big* money, and the more you pay, the less you play.

At this level, every parent is talking scholarships, and some are being led down a misguided path by less-than-fully-ethical club directors touting the latest and greatest head coach. Parents should be made aware that this situation can become "soccer hell" and the worst experience of both theirs and their child's life. Some, not all, of these coaches are involved in the big money leagues for two reasons: money and building a resume to get the next bigger and better job. More often than not, these teams are formed for both boys and girls at age 12, and by age 14, the team has changed so much that often the sponsoring town, who had three to four players on the team, is now sponsoring a team with one or no players from that town. Asked why, most parents will tell you that this is the route to take to have their son or daughter gain the exposure that is needed to be considered for a college scholarship.

The fact is that less than 8 percent of all the Premier players countrywide get any kind of financial assistance to play college soccer. That leaves over 90 percent playing for the love of the game – the real reason to play. Premier teams advertise that they go to this tourney and that tourney, and that the college coaches will be there watching. The truth is, the college coaches are there mostly to see the U-19 boys and girls. As a Premier coach I have never had a call from a college coach regarding a player. However, as a high school coach who has gotten five players scholarships, I sometimes get calls and letters concerning my high school players.

As you may recall, earlier I stated that this age group can be the most enjoyable and rewarding to coach. Why? Why is this group so much fun if you have to deal with all the pressure, competitive situations, and crazed parents who would like to fire coaches like George Steinbrenner fires managers? Because of the kids. The 13- to 14-year-old athletes are wonderful to teach. If given a chance, they will perform beyond your wildest expectations. One of my fondest memories came during the last game with the team that fired me (even though I didn't realize it at the time). It was late in the game, and I subbed in a sometime starter (a sometime sub player who was really coming into her own, even though the "parent group" wanted her cut). I put her in at left wing. With approximately two minutes left, a shot was taken on goal from our right wing. The ball scooted across the goal, and there all by herself was our left wing, Debbie, right in the position she should have been and touched the ball in for the winning goal. The look on her face made everything that happened afterwards a lot easier to take. When I attended her Bat Mitzvah, she told me she would always remember that game. I think she will. That's the fun of this age group – the kids. By this age, the kids understand the reason they are playing and really grasp the concept of competing as opposed to winning and losing.

Coaches are teachers who get to wear shorts and T-shirts all the time. You are instructing your class (team) in the finer aspects of sportsmanship, skill, fair play, determination, and competition. You are the link that these players have with the world of sport. You must convey to them every day the love of competition and the meaning of sportsmanship. It is your duty to help these players obtain the skill and know-how they will need to achieve in high school and beyond. You will be remembered more for the things you don't say than the things you do. The things you do out of habit will become the groundwork for your players' work ethics. Your actions will speak volumes over the most verbose dialogue, and your ability to handle defeat with grace and victory with humility will be forever etched in your players' minds and hearts. "It is better to be humbled in defeat than remember one moment of your greatest victory."

CHAPTER 7

50 Nifty Youth Soccer Drills

Key to Diagrams	
▲	attacking player/offensive player
●	defender
Ⓐ	neutral player or coach
✪	goalkeeper
▲	player in possession of the ball
→	path of the ball (when it is kicked to another player or shot on goal)
--→	direction of a player's movement without the ball or when jumping
↷	ball being kicked or thrown up in the air
ᴡᴡ▶	player dribbling the ball
⌂	cone
○	half-cone disk
⊥	bowling pin

Drill #1: Open-Space Demonstration

Objective: To help players recognize how easy it is to move through unoccupied spaces. Use this demonstration to build a base of knowledge about the use of space, and refer to it in later teachings.

Equipment Required: One ball, two game markers

Directions:

Level 1

1. Have players huddle in a group.
2. Place two markers on a line about 10 yards apart.
3. Ask one player to stand by one of the markers.
4. Ask that player to walk to the other marker.

Level 2

1. Repeat procedures 1 and 2 from Level 1.
2. Ask one player to stand by one of the markers with a ball.
3. Ask that player to dribble the ball to the other marker.

Level 3

1. Repeat procedures 1 and 2 from Level 1.
2. Ask one player to stand by one of the markers with a ball and another player to stand by the other marker.
3. Ask the player with the ball to pass the ball to the teammate who is standing by the other marker.

Points to Emphasize: You have demonstrated how uncomplicated it is to move, dribble, and pass through open space. Youth players will develop an understanding of space more thoroughly when you give a visual demonstration. Refer to this demonstration often when explaining effecting use of space in training and game situations.

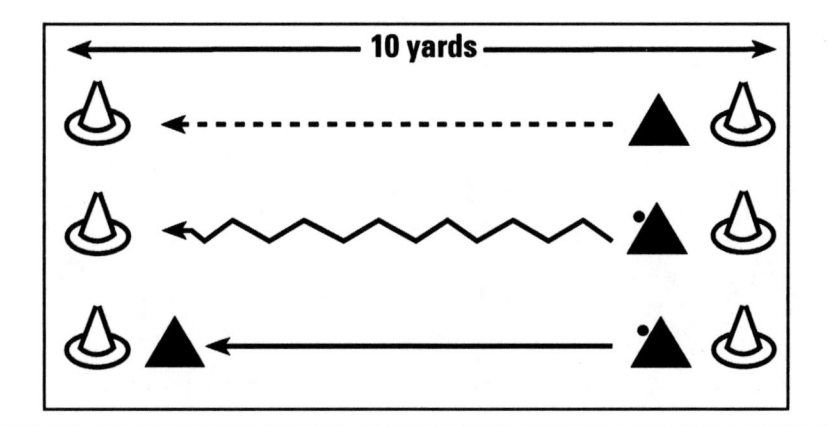

Drill #2: Closed-Space Demonstration

Objective: To demonstrate how impossible it is to move, dribble, and pass through closed spaces.

Equipment Required: One ball, two game markers

Directions:

Level 1

1. Have players huddled in a group.
2. Place two markers on a line about 10 yards apart.
3. Ask player A to stand by one of the markers.
4. Ask player B to stand on the line at a point midway between the markers.
5. Ask player A to walk on the line to the other marker.

Level 2

1. Repeat procedures 1 through 4 from Level 1, except player A has a ball.
2. Ask player A to dribble the ball to the opposite marker without going off the line.

Level 3

1. Repeat procedures 1 through 4 from Level 1, except player A has a ball.
2. Ask player C to stand by the unoccupied marker.
3. Ask player A to pass to player C.

Points to Emphasize: At Level 1 player A will find this task impossible because player B, who has closed the space between the two markers, has blocked his pathway. At Level 2 player A will not be able to dribble the ball through the space closed by player B. At Level 3 player A will not be able to pass the ball through the space closed by player B.

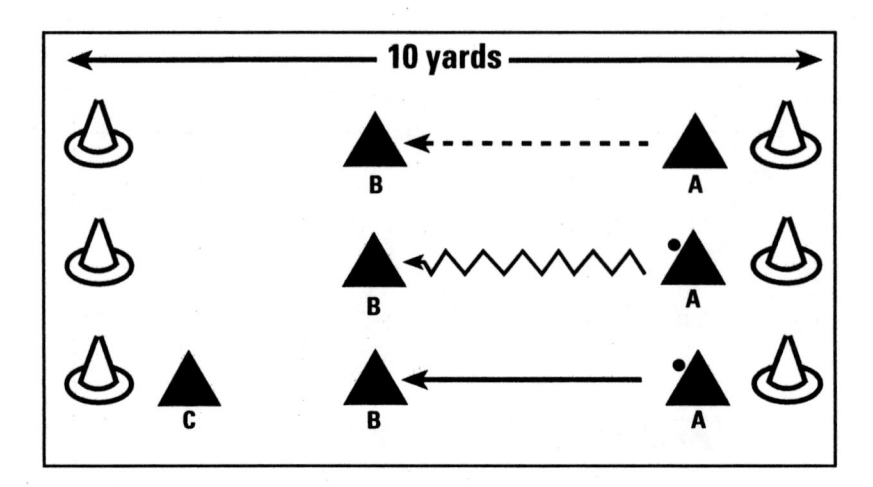

Developing an understanding of open versus closed space should be a top priority for youth players. Give them this visual demonstration of how impossible it is to move without the ball, to dribble, or to pass through closed spaces. Refer to this demonstration (see open space and closed space photos) when players begin clustering, colliding with teammates or opponents, or dribbling and passing into closed spaces. Explain to them the alternative, which is, of course, to use open space.

Open Space

Closed Space

Drill #3: Personal-Space Demonstration

Objective: To help develop an understanding that personal space is the space that immediately surrounds players and is affected by player movement.

Equipment Required: Nine game markers

Directions:

1. Place five players each into four grids, each five yards by five yards. Number the grids 1 through 4.
2. Ask the players to move freely through their grids.
3. If a player touches another player, he is frozen.
4. Ask players from grid number 2 to join the players from grid number 1 and the players from 3 to join the players from grid number 4.
5. At this point, all frozen players become unfrozen and rejoin the other players.
6. Ask the players to move freely in their grids for about 30 seconds.
7. Finally, have all of the players move to grid number 1.
8. Ask the players to move freely for about 30 seconds, reminding them not to touch anyone as they move.

Points to Emphasize: As the players move in a grid with only four other players, maintaining their personal space should not be challenging. As the number of players in a space increases, movement becomes more difficult. When all the players are moving in a small space, it becomes almost impossible to maintain or not invade someone else's personal space. This drill can serve as a visual reminder for players during scrimmages and games of how difficult movement becomes when they cluster. Hopefully, the result will be better spacing and less swarming so that players can maintain personal spaces.

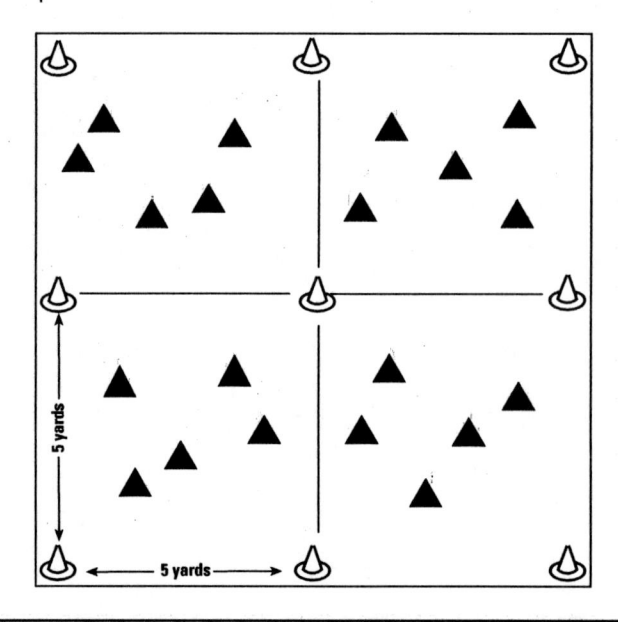

Drill #4: General-Space Demonstration

Objective: To help develop an understanding that general space is the entire area in which a player can function and that within this general space, larger spaces are easier to negotiate than smaller ones.

Equipment Required: Eight game markers

Directions:

1. Have all players scattered in a grid identified by four game markers approximately 20 yards apart.
2. Ask them to move freely through the entire grid.
3. Expand the size of the grid to 50 yards by 50 yards.
4. Ask the players to move freely through the larger grid.
5. After the players move in both grids, discuss with them in which grid they found it easier to move.

Points to Emphasize: The personal-space demonstration showed how increasing the number of players in a space affected a player's personal space and movement. This drill demonstrates how increasing the size of the space makes player movement easier because there is more time to make decisions about changing direction, speed, and level. Players should recognize that by using all the spaces within the general space properly, they can maintain field balance and move more freely.

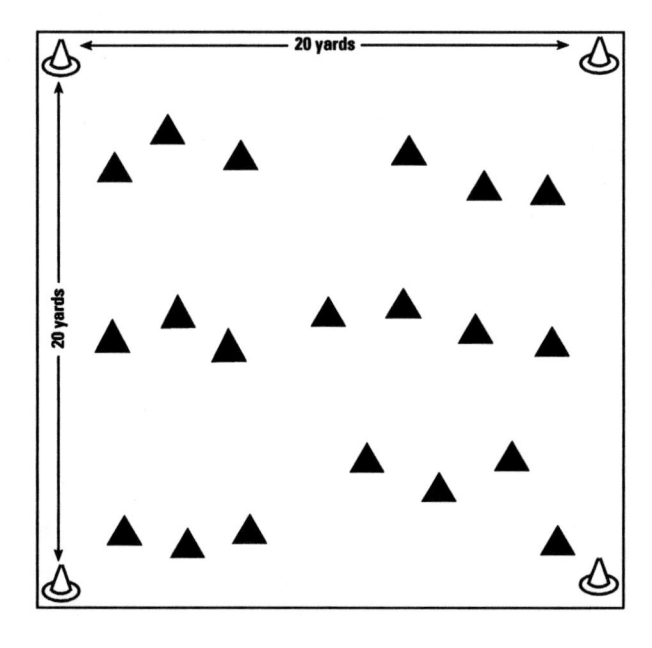

Drill #5: Fancy-Footwork Drill

Objective: To improve the ability to control the ball while in a stationary position with no defensive pressure.

Equipment Required: One soccer ball for each player, four game markers

Directions:

1. Scatter players with a ball in a 20-yard-by-20-yard grid.
2. While stationary, players practice controlled touches on the ball.
3. Players can combine these touches in various ways to change speed, direction, or level. Encourage players to change the position of the ball in relationship to the body with pushaways, pullbacks, rollovers, and so forth.
4. Next, have the players change body position in relationship to the ball with stepovers, scissors, walkovers, and so forth.

Points to Emphasize: There should be time for hundreds of touches on the ball during each practice. Encourage players to explore ways to move the ball using the inside, outside, sole, and heel of each foot. Players may mirror individual moves demonstrated by coaches, but you should encourage them to create new combinations of moves. As they touch the ball, encourage them to maintain good vision constantly. For variety and to reduce fatigue, use partners. Have one partner work on skills for a minute and then give the ball to the partner. Repeat. Change formations using triangles, circles, and so forth to add variety to this drill. It is essential that you give players time to develop these skills from a stationary position without movement into other spaces and without defensive pressure. Players should practice these moves at home as part of a daily routine.

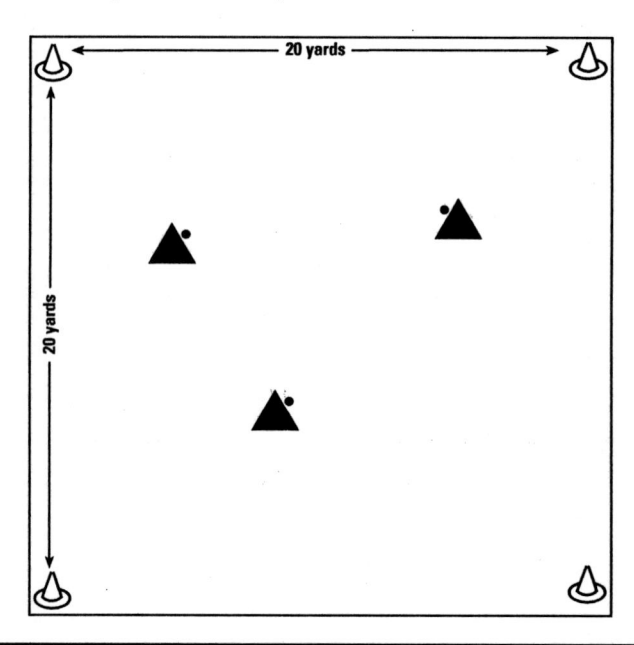

Drill #6: Follow the Leader

Objective: To develop dribbling skills while negotiating space with no defensive pressure.

Equipment Required: One soccer ball for each player, four game markers

Directions:

1. Divide group into lines of four or five players in a 20-yard-by-20-yard grid.
2. The first player in line is the leader and begins moving through the grid with the rest of the players following while dribbling their balls.
3. On the coach's signal, the last person in line will push his ball out approximately five yards in front of the leader, sprint after it, and become the new leader.
4. The new last person will repeat this action on the next whistle.

Points to Emphasize: Coaches should encourage ball control by discussing the relationships of touching the ball with various parts of the foot and proper use of the general space provided so that the lines don't move into the same space. As players become more controlled in their movements, coaches should allow players to do this drill without their signals.

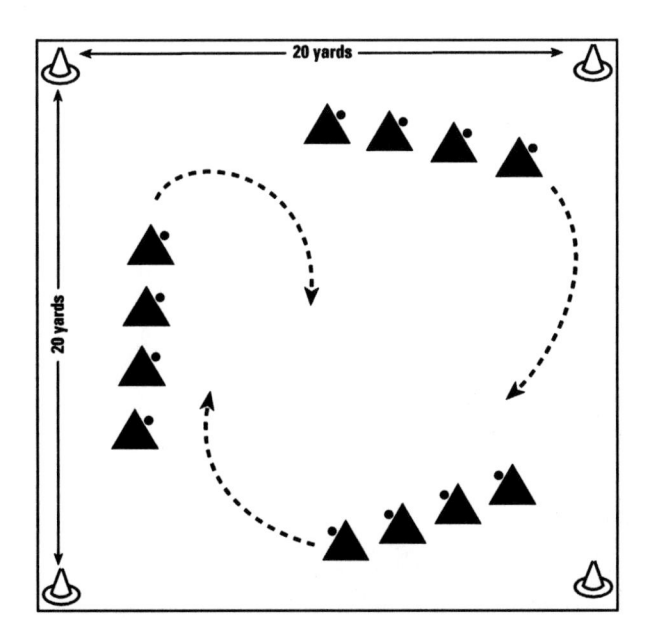

Drill #7: Freedom Drill

Objective: To develop dribbling skills while negotiating space with no defensive pressure.

Equipment Required: One soccer ball for every two players, five game markers

Directions:

1. Space partners around a circle approximately 30 yards in diameter.
2. On the coach's whistle, the partner with the ball travels into the circle, practicing his individual moves as he encounters other players who are doing likewise.
3. After a minute of moving, the player with the ball returns and gives the ball to his partner, who repeats the action.
4. Players have complete freedom to use any of their individual moves during this drill.

Points to Emphasize: Encourage players to use a variety of individual moves to change directions, speeds, and levels as they negotiate space. Refer to the demonstration on space and movement concepts if players are moving into closed spaces. This drill is the next step in the dribbling progression because it requires using individual moves to travel through space. The drill allows players the freedom to develop skills without defensive pressure.

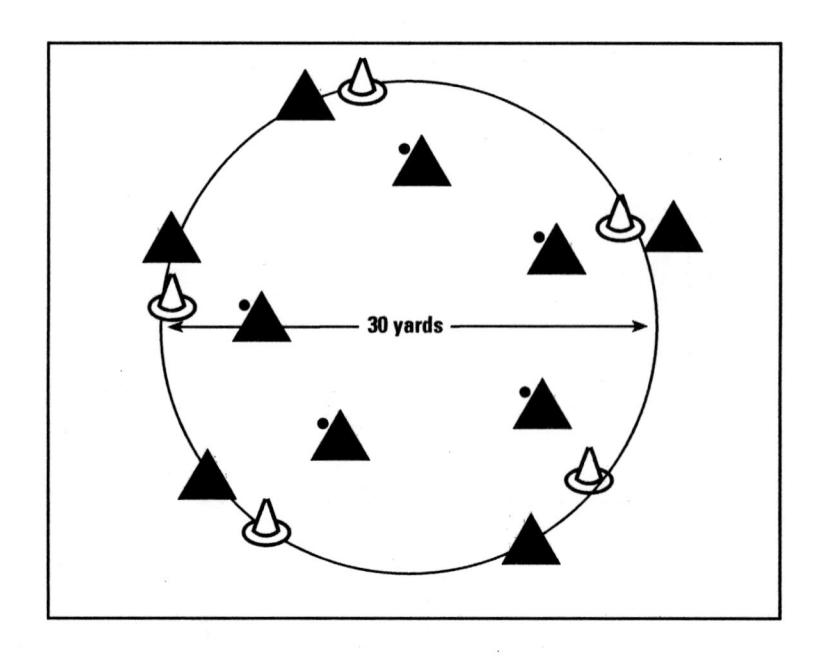

Drill #8: Freeze Drill

Objective: To develop dribbling skills while negotiating space with no defensive pressure.

Equipment Required: One soccer ball for each player, four game markers

Directions:

1. Scatter players in a 20-yard-by-20-yard grid.
2. All players move freely with a ball through the grid.
3. When the coach signals by blowing a whistle, the players must freeze by bringing their balls to a complete stop.
4. Variations of this drill might include touching the ball with any body part on one side of the body, freezing on a specific number of body parts, or freezing at various levels.

Points to Emphasize: This drill allows players to develop individual moves while negotiating space without defensive pressure. Encourage players to use body parts on their nondominant side. Freezing at various levels might include straight leg, crouched, or kneeling positions.

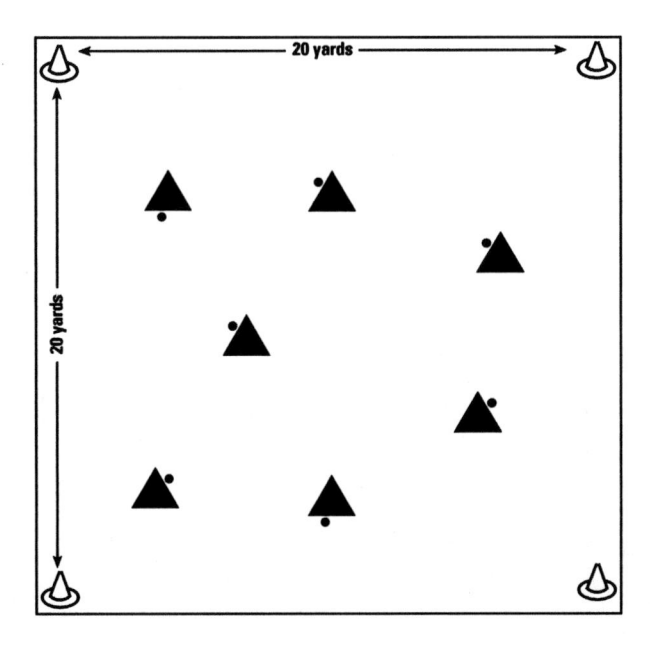

Drill #9: Sprint Drill

Objective: To develop dribbling skills and speed while negotiating space with no defensive pressure.

Equipment Required: One soccer ball for each player, four game markers

Directions:

1. Scatter players in a 20-yard-by-20-yard grid with a ball.
2. The players travel through the grid until they hear the coach's whistle.
3. On that signal, players dribble their balls as fast as they can out of the grid.
4. They continue dribbling as fast as they can until they hear a second whistle.
5. Then the players dribble as fast as they can back to the grid, where they continue traveling through the grid at a moderate pace.

Points to Emphasize: Present this drill only when players have developed sufficient ball control skills. Encourage them to push the ball away to open spaces at a distance of five to seven yards and then sprint to the ball. Kicking the ball as far as they can and sprinting after it is not the purpose of this drill.

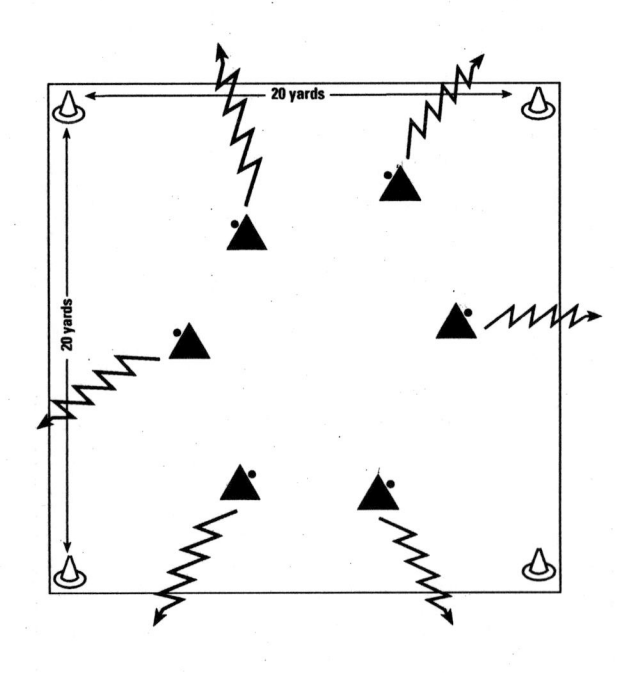

Drill #10: Circle Dribble Tag

Objective: To help develop dribbling skills while under subtle defensive pressure.

Equipment Required: Two soccer balls and four game markers for every six players

Directions:

Level 1
1. Place six players in a 10-yard-by-10-yard grid.
2. Four players form a circle.
3. Two players, each with a ball, stand outside the circle on opposite sides.
4. Designate one of these players as the tagger.
5. On the coach's signal, the tagger has 30 seconds to catch the other player with a ball while both players are dribbling.
6. The tagger may cut through the circle, but the player being chased may not.

Level 2
1. Repeat Level 1 procedures 1 through 6.
2. While the tagger is chasing the other player, teammates who have formed the circle move as a unit to shield the player being chased from the tagger.

Points to Emphasize: Players need to use good visual habits to know when the tagger has changed directions. Changing directions and speeds frequently will help the player being chased.

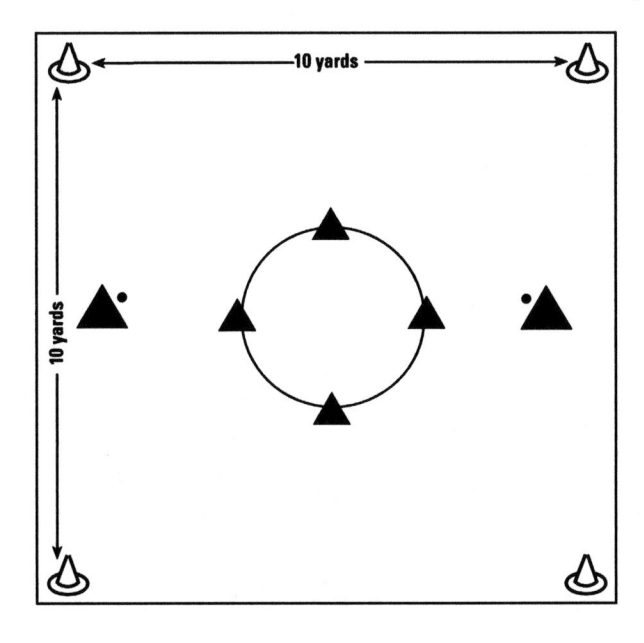

Drill #11: Shake-and-Take Drill

Objective: To develop dribbling skills used to create space and go to goal with defensive pressure.

Equipment Required: One soccer ball for each player, one marker for each goal, four goals

Directions:

Level 1
1. Place a marker 40 yards from the goal.
2. A player dribbles toward the marker, executes an individual move to create space (a scissors move, for example), and then goes to the goal and shoots.

Level 2
1. Place two markers 40 yards from goal about 5 yards apart.
2. A defender stands on a line between the markers and tries to tackle the ball away from the attacker as he attempts to go between the markers to the goal.

Level 3
1. Player A stands 40 yards from the goal.
2. A defender stands 30 yards from the goal.
3. The ball is passed to player A.
4. When player A touches the ball the defender may pursue him.
5. Player A uses individual moves to create space to go to the goal.

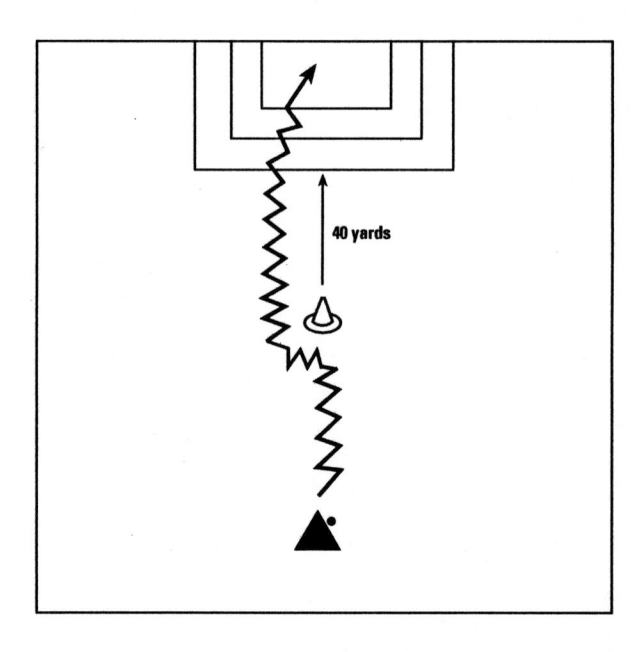

Points to Emphasize: All players should work to develop individual moves with imaginary pressure (the marker in Level 1) until they experience success. When their skills have improved to the point where they need more challenge, add a defender who can move only laterally (Level 2). This will add subtle pressure. A defender applies game-like pressure at Level 3. Do not rush players through their progressions. Use as many goals as are available, or make temporary goals, so players have many opportunities.

White jersey player has avoided dark jersey defender and is now on the move offensively.

Drill #12: Sprint Challenge Drill

Objective: To develop dribbling skills and speed when confronted with game-like defensive pressure.

Equipment Required: One soccer ball for every three players, four goals

Directions:

Level 1
1. Player A stands about five yards behind player B.
2. The coach passes the ball forward.
3. Player B must collect the ball, sprint toward the goal, and shoot before the defender can catch him.
4. Variations include serving balls at various speeds, directions, and levels.

Level 2
1. Repeat Level 1 procedures 1 through 4.
2. Repeat the action, but add a goalkeeper to increase the defensive pressure.

Points to Emphasize: Encourage players to push the ball five to seven yards to maintain both speed and control. When adding a goalkeeper, restrict him by not allowing him to come off the goal line. As skills increase, add more goalkeeping pressure.

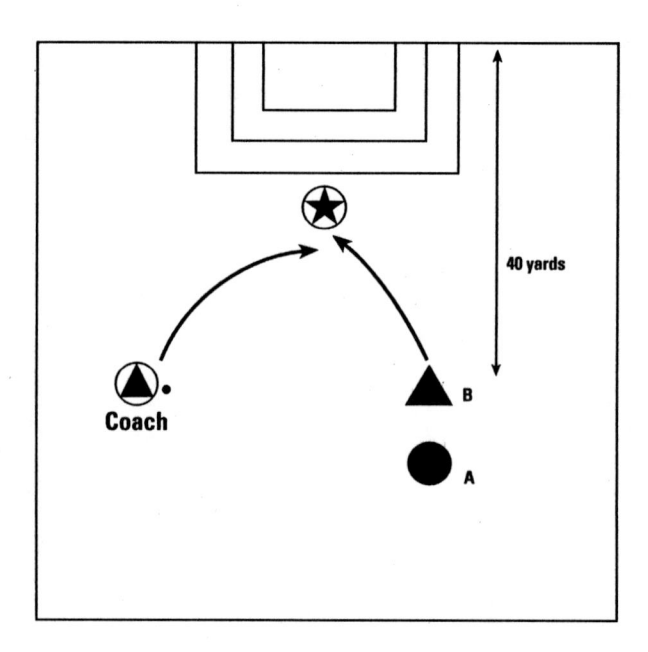

Drill #13: Partner Dribble Game

Objective: To help develop dribbling skills to create space with game-like defensive pressure.

Equipment Required: One soccer ball and four game markers for every two players

Directions:

1. In a 10-yard-by-10-yard grid, one partner stands on a line with a ball and the other partner stands on the opposite side of the square.
2. Player A passes the ball to player B.
3. When player B receives the ball, player A pursues him in an effort to close his space and touch the ball or force him out of the grid.
4. If player A touches the ball, he earns 1 point.
5. If player B can dribble safely to the opposite line, he earns 2 points.
6. The first player to earn 6 points is the winner.
7. Then, they reverse roles.

Points to Emphasize: The offensive player in this drill earns more points for being successful because this is an offensive drill. Encourage the offensive player to use a variety of moves to create space.

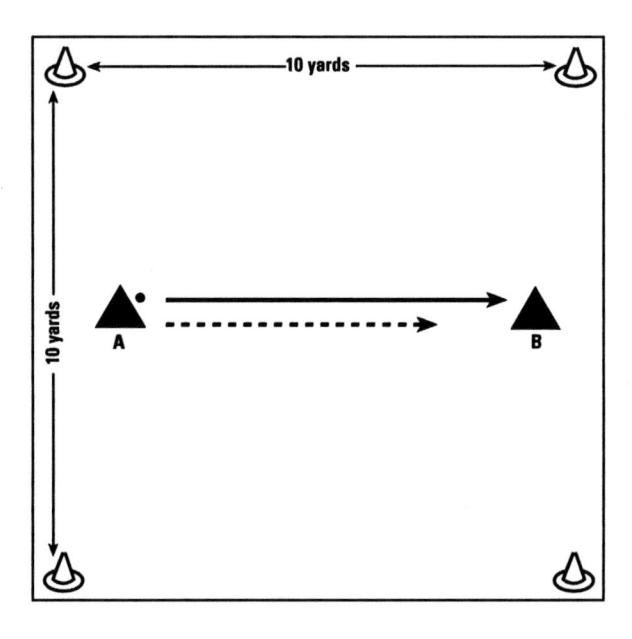

Drill #14: Force Challenge Drill

Objective: To help develop an understanding of the application of force when passing the ball.

Equipment Required: One soccer ball for every two players

Directions:

1. Players stand approximately five yards from the sideline.
2. Ask players to kick the ball so that it stops on the line.
3. Repeat several times.
4. Request players to repeat this action from 10-, 20-, and 30-yard distances.
5. Use partners to retrieve balls.

Points to Emphasize: Discuss the proportional relationship between leg speed and the distance the ball will travel. Encourage players to use proper kicking technique for making flat passes.

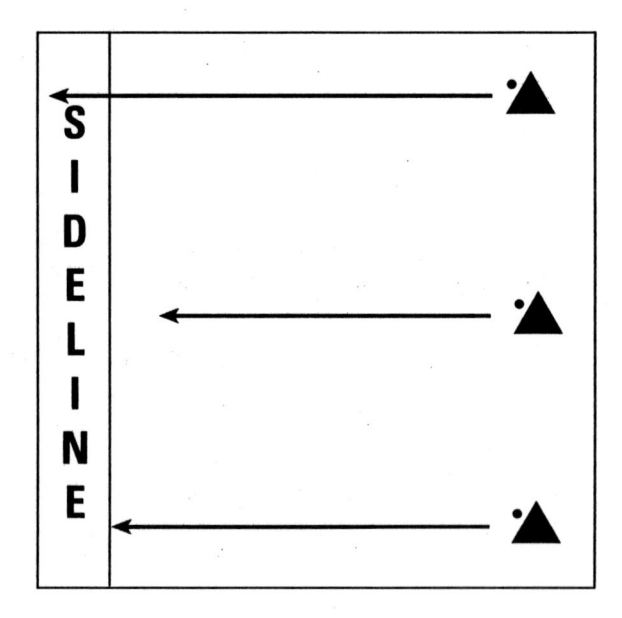

Drill #15: Partner Passing Drill

Objective: To help develop passing accuracy and collection skills from a stationary passer to a stationary target with no defensive pressure.

Equipment Required: One soccer ball for every two players, four game markers

Directions:

Level 1
1. Position players in a scattered formation in a 30-yard-by-30-yard grid.
2. Partners should be about 10 yards apart.
3. Players will pass to their partners, who will collect the ball and return the pass.
4. Encourage players to speak aloud the sequence of collect, look, look right, and pass.
5. Repeat looking left, or combining left and right, before returning the pass.

Level 2
1. Repeat Level 1 procedures 1 through 5.
2. Vary this activity by using three players in a triangle or several players in a circle formation.
3. After a stationary player passes to a stationary target, he may run to that player's space.

Points to Emphasize: It is important for beginning players to stop the ball before returning it to their partners. Encourage players to relax the part of the body used for stopping the ball as this will have a cushioning effect. By stopping the ball, players will improve the accuracy of passes because it's easier to strike a stationary ball than one in motion. Level 2 incorporates movement after the pass. This will help to establish the philosophy that the passer should continue to be a player instead of becoming a spectator after passing. Later this movement will lead to executing wall passes.

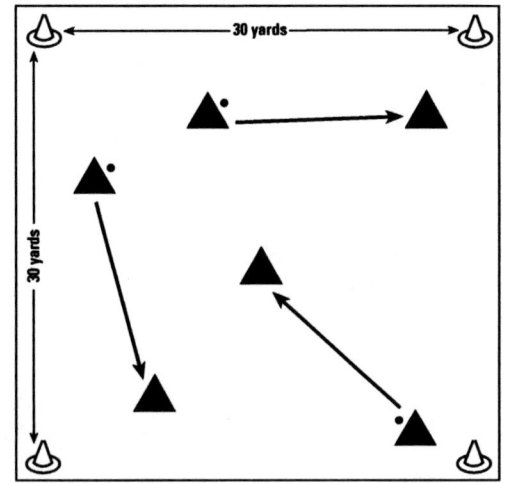

Drill #16: Thread-the-Needle Drill

Objective: To help improve passing accuracy and collection skills from a stationary passer to a stationary target with no defensive pressure.

Equipment Required: One soccer ball and two game markers for every two players

Directions:

1. Scatter partners with two cones between them.
2. Place cones initially about three or four yards apart.
3. Instruct players to pass to each other by having the ball go between the markers.
4. Have some fun with this drill by making it a game.
5. On the coach's signal, players begin passing.
6. After each successful pass, they take one step backward.
7. If the ball does not go between the markers, players must return to the starting point and begin again.
8. After two minutes stop and see how far apart partners are.

Points to Emphasize: Begin this drill with partners approximately 10 yards apart. As the skill level of the players improves, increase the distance between the players and decrease the distance between the markers. To assess player performance, count how many times the players are able to pass the ball between the markers in 20 attempts. Insure that players are collecting and bringing the ball to a stop before returning the pass.

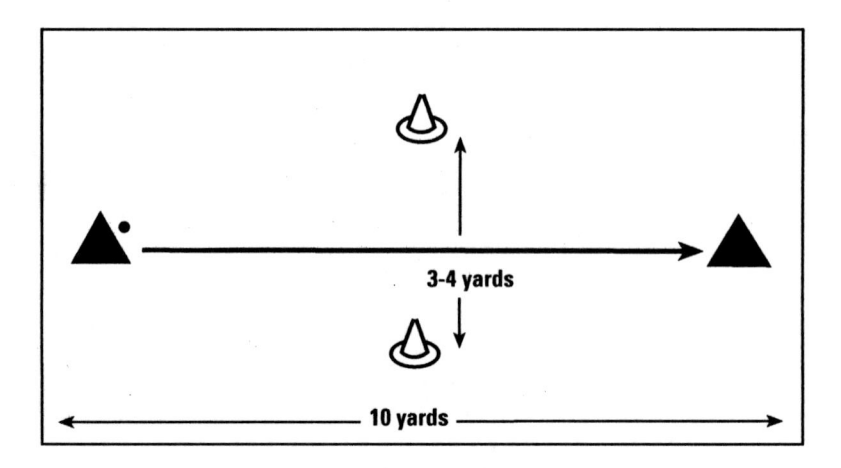

Drill #17: Tunnel Connection Drill

Objective: To help improve passing accuracy and collection skills from a stationary passer to a stationary target with no defensive pressure.

Equipment Required: One soccer ball for every three players

Directions:

1. Three players stand in a line approximately 10 yards apart.
2. Player A passes the ball through player B's legs to player C.
3. Player B then switches with player A.
4. Player C passes through player A's legs to player B and then switches with player A.
5. Repeat action several times.

Points to Emphasize: Encourage players to collect and wait for their partners to get to their positions before passing. Without patience, spacing becomes a problem with this drill. If necessary, place markers at 10-yard intervals to help players with spacing.

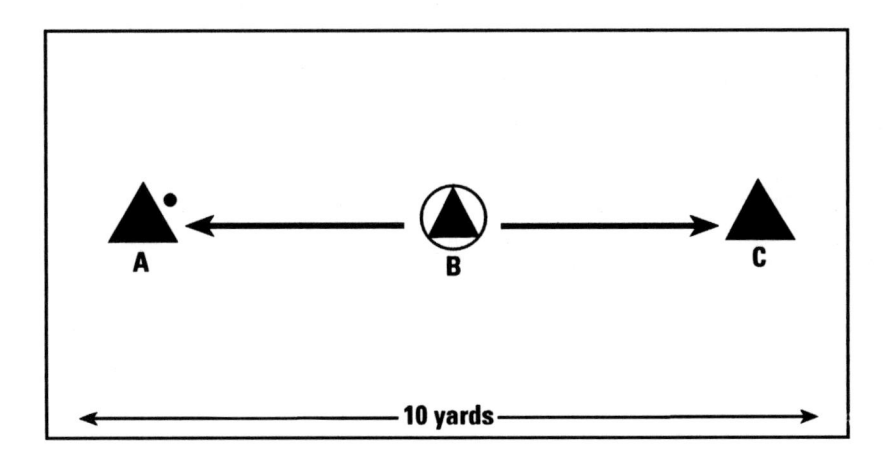

Drill #18: Good-bye Drill

Objective: To help develop passing accuracy and collection skills from a stationary passer to a stationary target and initiate movement after the pass with no defensive pressure.

Equipment Required: One soccer ball and four game markers for every three players

Directions:

Level 1
1. Position three players in a 10-yard-by-10-yard grid so that they each occupy a corner of the grid.
2. Player A will pass to player B, then say good-bye, and travel to the unoccupied corner of the grid.
3. Player B then passes to player C, says good-bye, and travels to the corner vacated by player A.
4. Repeat this action several times.

Level 2
1. After players feel comfortable with the spacing provided by the 10-yard grid, remove the game markers.
2. Request that all players travel in threes, repeating the movement in general space.

Points to Emphasize: Encourage players to deliver crisp, flat passes that will be easy to collect. Players should pass and move quickly to the open space. Reinforce this repeated action of pass and move in scrimmages and games. At Level 2, encourage players to move through open spaces as they negotiate other players and maintain 10-yard spacing.

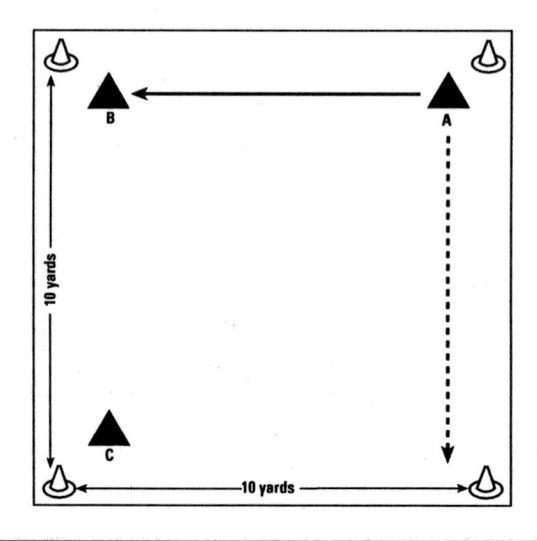

Drill #19: Circle Collection Drill

Objective: To help develop passing accuracy and collection skills from stationary passer to moving target with no defensive pressure.

Equipment Required: Soccer balls for every player

Directions:

1. Six players form a circle.
2. Each player has a ball.
3. Three players are in constant motion inside the circle.
4. As an inside player makes eye contact with a player on the circle, the ball is passed to him.
5. He returns the pass to the player who passed it and moves to another space to collect another pass.
6. Players forming the circle exchange places every one to two minutes.

Points to Emphasize: Caution moving players inside the circle to pass through open spaces. Players on the inside should collect, look, and make a good decision concerning their next pass.

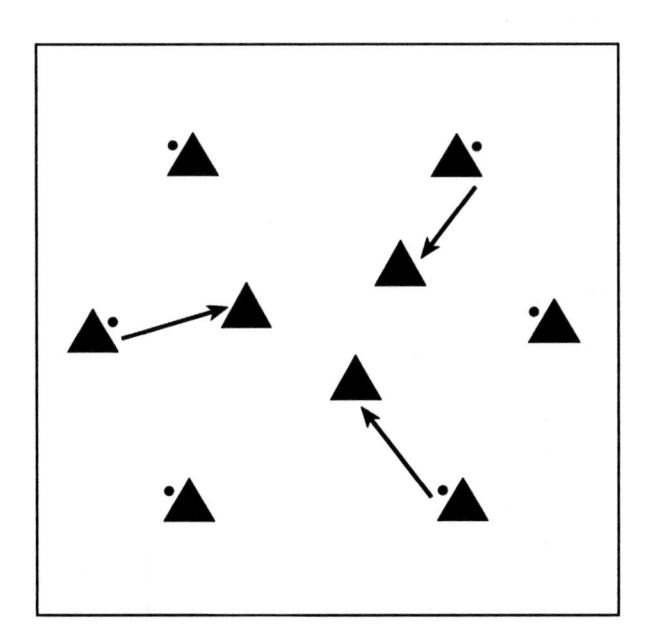

Drill #20: Hello Drill

Objective: To help develop passing accuracy and collection skills from a stationary passer to a moving target with no defensive pressure.

Equipment Required: One soccer ball and four game markers for every three players

Directions:

Level 1
1. Position three players, each in a corner of a 10-yard-by-10-yard grid.
2. Player C, closest to the unoccupied corner and not in possession of the ball, will move to the unoccupied corner and say the word "hello."
3. Player A, with the ball, passes to player C.
4. Player B then moves to the space vacated by player C to receive a pass from player C.

Level 2
1. As players become comfortable with spacing, remove game markers. Have several groups of players moving in one large grid repeating Level 1 action.

Points to Emphasize: Coaches should encourage players moving to space to give an oral reminder to the passer. In this drill, they should be saying "hello." For the sake of consistency, coaches may want their players to say the word "space." Moving players should wait until the passer has controlled the ball and has made eye contact before initiating any movement. Discuss with players how delivering a soft pass to a player coming toward the ball will aid the collection process.

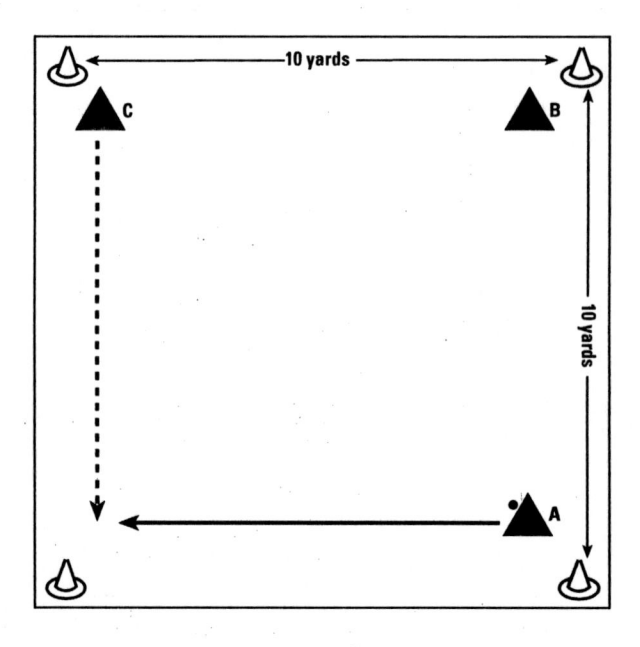

Drill #21: Spaceman Drill

Objective: To help develop passing accuracy and collection skills from a stationary passer to a moving target with no defensive pressure.

Equipment Required: One soccer ball and three game markers for every two players

Directions:

Level 1
1. Position two players in a triangle identified by markers placed 10 yards apart.
2. Each player occupies a corner of the triangle.
3. The player without the ball runs to the unoccupied corner of the triangle and says loudly the word "space."
4. The player with the ball passes it to the moving player.
5. The player who passed the ball moves to the unoccupied corner to receive a return pass.
6. Repeat this action several times.

Level 2
1. Remove game markers. Have partners travel through general space using a triangular pattern with 10-yard spacing.

Points to Emphasize: Encourage the player moving to open space to make eye contact with the passer to insure that the passer has the ball in control to make a pass. Instruct the passer to lead the player moving to space by passing the ball slightly ahead of him so he doesn't have to break stride to collect the ball. Timing runs and communicating well are important to the success of this drill.

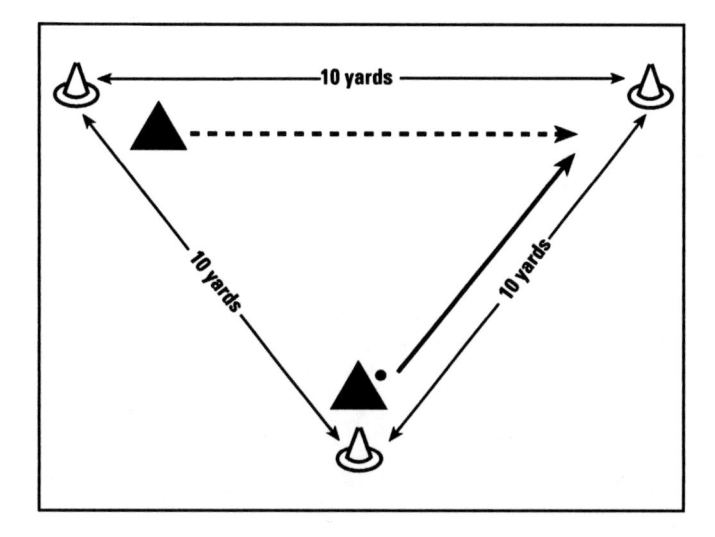

Drill #22: Diagonal Passing Drill

Objective: To develop passing accuracy and collection skills from a moving passer to a stationary target with no defensive pressure.

Equipment Required: One soccer ball and four game markers for every three players

Directions:

Level 1
1. Position three players in a 10-yard-by-10-yard grid so that each occupies a corner space.
2. Player A dribbles to the unoccupied corner and passes diagonally to player B.
3. Player B dribbles to the corner vacated by player A and passes to player C.
4. Repeat action several times.

Level 2
1. Remove the game markers.
2. Have players move through general space repeating this action.

Points to Emphasize: A player must use a controlled dribble to keep the ball in the grid. He must turn his nonkicking foot slightly toward the target before passing. This will allow the hips to rotate and the kicking foot to swing outside of the ball before impact. At Level 2, encourage players to maintain 10-yard spacing and avoid closed spaces.

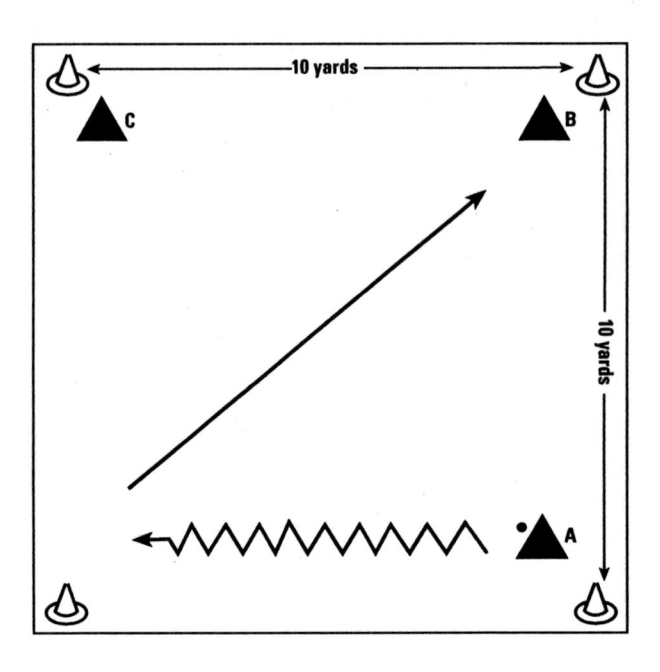

Drill #23: Return-to-Sender Drill

Objective: To help develop passing accuracy and collection skills from a moving passer to a stationary target with no defensive pressure.

Equipment Required: One soccer ball for every two players, four game markers, two sets of jerseys — one jersey for each player

Directions:

1. Scatter players in a 30-yard-by-30-yard grid.
2. Divide the group into two equal teams with different jerseys.
3. The players with striped jerseys, each with a ball, move freely in a grid.
4. As they approach a stationary player with a solid-colored jersey, they will pass to him, collect the return pass, and then move through space, finding another solid-colored team member to whom they will pass.
5. Repeat for one minute, making as many passes as possible to different players.
6. Then, reverse roles.
7. Vary this drill by delivering passes at different levels.

Points to Emphasize: This drill will go more smoothly for beginning players if the stationary players collect the ball with their hands and then roll it to the passer, who should be moving to a new space. As the players become more skillful, require them to collect with various body parts or execute one-touch passes.

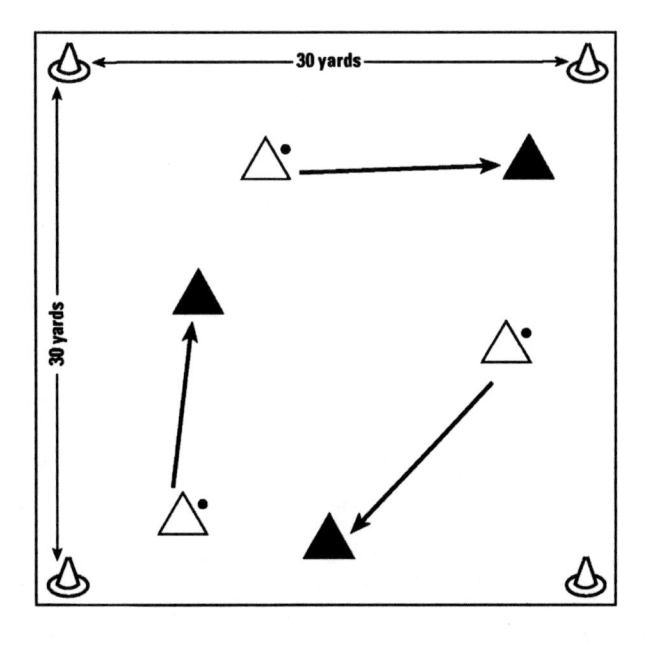

Drill #24: Four-Corner Passing Drill

Objective: To help develop passing accuracy and collection skills from a moving passer to a moving target with no defensive pressure.

Equipment Required: One soccer ball and four game markers for every five players

Directions:

1. Position players in a 10-yard-by-10-yard grid so that players occupy the corners of the grid.
2. Player E will be outside the grid beside player A, ready to occupy that space when player A leaves.
3. Player A moves toward, and passes to, player B, who begins to move when player A reaches the halfway point between them.
4. After passing to player B, player A continues to move and occupies player B's original space.
5. Player B collects on the move and passes to player C, who begins to move when player B reaches the halfway point between them.
6. Players continue this action of collecting while moving, passing to the next player, and then occupying his corner of the grid.
7. As passing skills improve, challenge players by counting how many times they can pass the ball around the entire grid in two minutes.

Points to Emphasize: Passers should make eye contact with players they are passing to and should lead them with a pass that they can easily collect. You may use more players in this drill by positioning them by the corners outside the grid. As a player completes the pass, he would then go to the end of the line instead of standing by the marker.

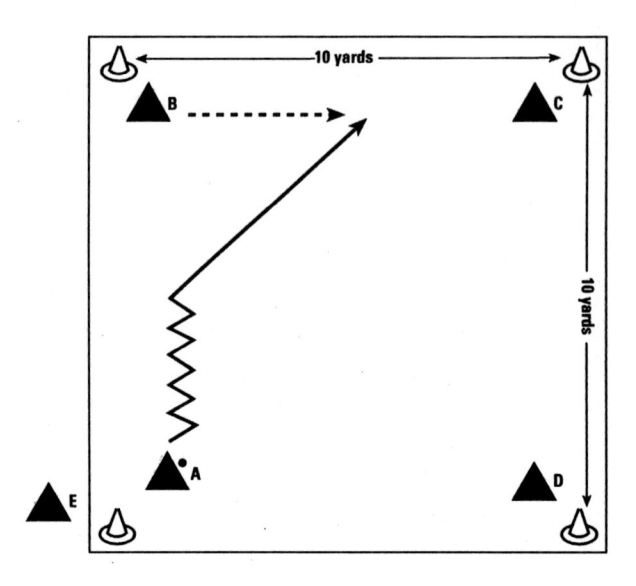

Drill #25: Pass-Dribble-Pass Drill

Objective: To help develop passing accuracy and collection skills from a moving passer to a moving target with no defensive pressure.

Equipment Required: One soccer ball and four game markers for every two players

Directions:

Level 1
1. Position two players in a 15-yard-by-15-yard grid.
2. Player A will pass to player B, who dribbles into open space and then turns and passes back to player A, who has moved to a new space behind him.
3. Repeat this action.

Level 2
1. Remove game markers
2. Players repeat action moving in general space.

Points to Emphasize: This drill requires players to pass the ball in a backward direction. Players taking space behind another player should communicate that they are in an open space by saying the word "drop." Players passing in a backward direction should begin developing the use of the heel to pass and changing the position of their body in relation to the ball as demonstrated on the stepover move. At Level 2 encourage partners to communicate. With all partner groups moving in general space, partners sometimes become separated without this communication.

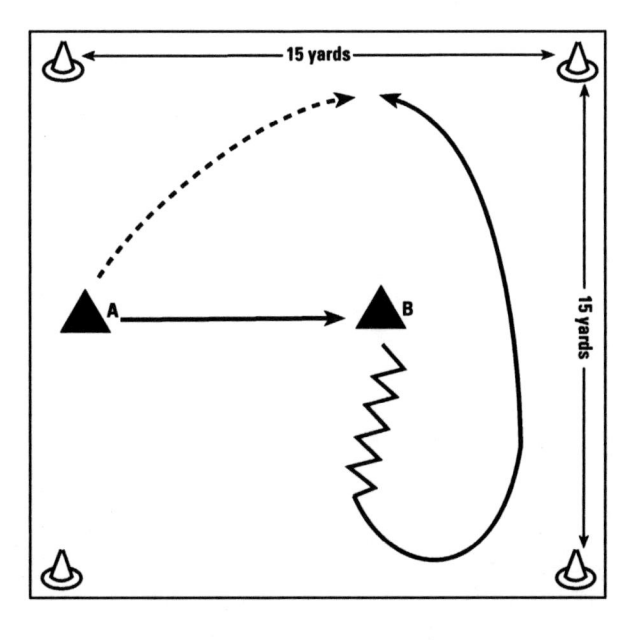

Drill #26: First-Touch Drill

Objective: To help develop passing accuracy from a moving passer to a moving target with no defensive pressure.

Equipment Required: One soccer ball for every two players and four game markers

Directions:

1. Scatter players in pairs in a 20-yard-by-20-yard grid.
2. Each set of partners has a ball.
3. On the coach's signal, the players begin to move through the grid.
4. The players with the ball pass to their partners, who must pass back on the first touch.
5. Partners continue moving using only one-touch passing.

Points to Emphasize: Players must use good visual habits in negotiating space to avoid other players. Initially partners should move with spacing no more than three or four yards apart. As they become more proficient with their one-touch passing, they can separate by greater distances.

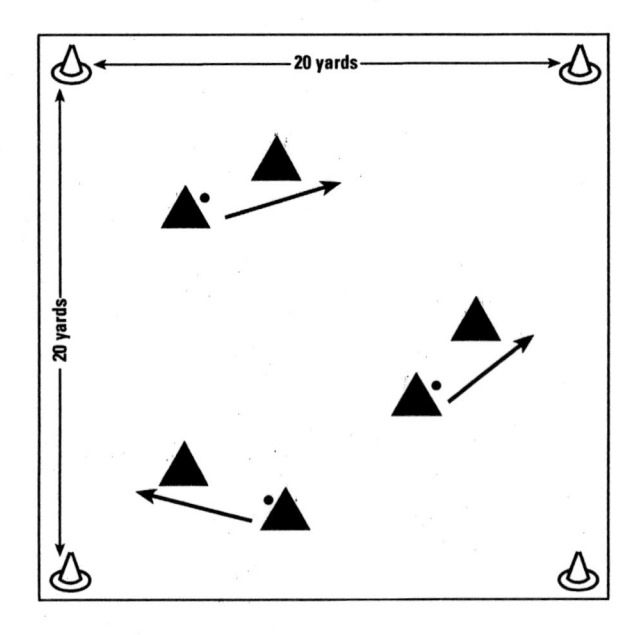

Drill #27: Star Drill

Objective: To help develop passing and collection skills with subtle defensive pressure.

Equipment Required: One soccer ball for every six players

Directions:

1. Position five players to form points of a star.
2. Place one defender in the middle of the star.
3. Challenge players to make as many consecutive passes as possible without losing control or allowing the defender to touch the ball.
4. Do not allow players to pass the ball to players beside them.

Points to Emphasize: This is a five-versus-one drill. The offensive players have a big advantage. Beginning players need this advantage to collect, look, and make good decisions with the ball.

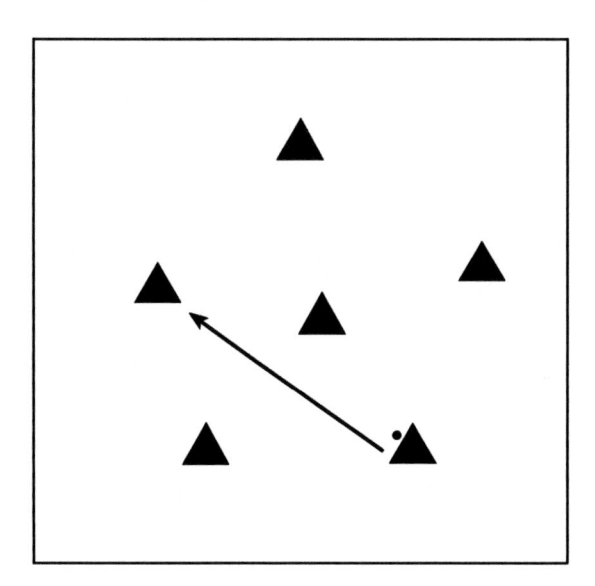

Drill #28: Monkey-in-the-Middle Drill

Objective: To help develop passing and collection skills with subtle pressure, movement without the ball, and decision-making ability concerning the use of open versus closed space.

Equipment Required: One soccer ball and four game markers for every four players

Directions:

1. Players occupy spaces by three of the markers.
2. A fourth player is in the middle and is affectionately referred to as the "monkey."
3. The perimeter players are playing a three-versus-one keepaway game.
4. They are not allowed to pass the ball across the middle of the square.
5. This forces them to move constantly to support positions so the player with the ball always has two passing lanes from which to choose.
6. For example, if the ball is by cone A, players would support in spaces by cone B and cone D.
7. If the player in the middle, the defender, closes the space between A and B, then the pass is made to the player at cone D.
8. Then support positioning would go to cone A and cone C.
9. Since a player already occupies cone A, the player who was at cone B would move to cone C to support.
10. It is impossible for the defender to close both passing lanes.
11. The defender earns his way out of the middle by touching the ball or forcing an error in passing or collecting.

Points to Emphasize: Perimeter players must collect, look, and make a decision about passing choices. Perimeter players must communicate with each other concerning space. Variations might include limiting touches on the ball, using diagonal runs to space, or allowing dribbling to space.

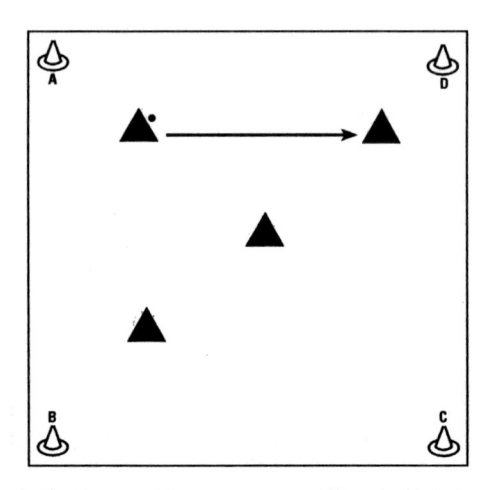

Drill #29: Cone Drill

Objective: To help develop passing and collection skills with game-like defensive pressure.

Equipment Required: One soccer ball and five game markers for every six players

Directions:

1. Position a player on each side of a 15-yard-by-15-yard grid.
2. One player has a ball.
3. Place a game marker in the center of the grid.
4. Two players are inside the grid.
5. One is an offensive player; the other is a defensive player.
6. The offensive player must run around the cone and sprint toward the player with the ball.
7. The player with the ball passes to the offensive player if he is in an open space.
8. If the defender closes his space, the passer passes instead to another player on the grid.
9. The offensive player repeats, going around the cone toward the new player with the ball.
10. The offensive player collects and returns the ball each time to the passer, who then passes to another player on the perimeter of the grid.

Points to Emphasize: Challenge players to count how many times the offensive player receives a pass in one minute. Passers must give the offensive players soft passes to collect. Defensive players work hard to close the space between the offensive player and the passer. Vary the degree of difficulty for collection by serving balls at various speeds and levels to challenge more advanced players.

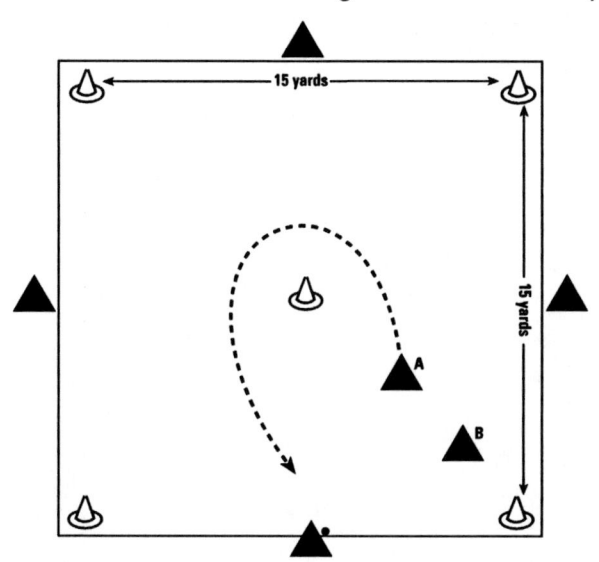

Drill #30: Check-Out/Check-In Drill

Objective: To help develop passing and collection skills with game-like defensive pressure.

Equipment Required: One soccer ball and four game markers for every six players

Directions:

1. Position a player on each side of a 15-yard-by-15-yard grid.
2. One player has the ball.
3. Two players are inside the grid.
4. Player A runs away (checks out) from the ball, changes direction, and then sprints toward the ball (checks in) to receive a pass.
5. If the defender (player B) closes the space, the passer plays the ball to another player on the grid.
6. If the offensive player collects the pass, he should shield the ball for 5 to 10 seconds before returning a pass.
7. Challenge players to count how many consecutive passes the offensive player receives in one minute without the defensive player touching the ball.

Points to Emphasize: Offensive players should move away from the ball at a moderate rate of speed. After changing directions, they should accelerate toward the ball. Changing speeds makes denying space more difficult for the defender.

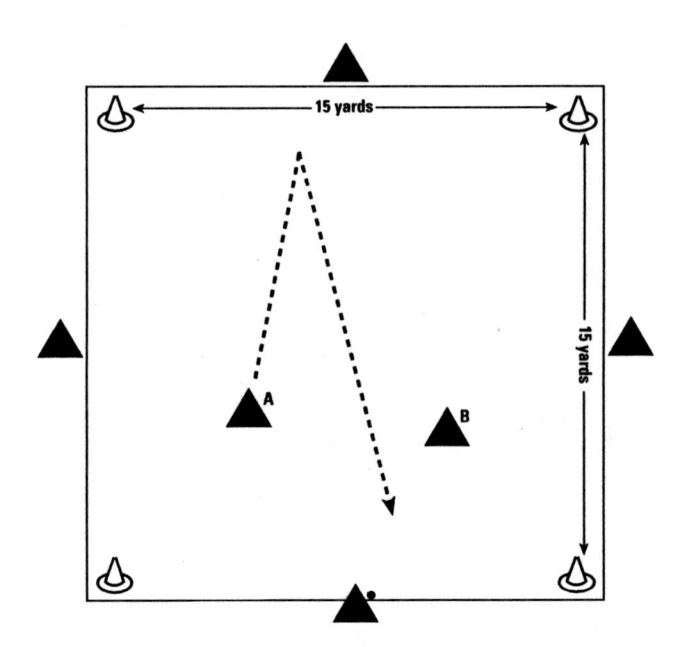

Drill #31: Three-Versus-Two Drill

Objective: To help develop decision-making abilities concerning passing choices with game-like defensive pressure.

Equipment Required: One soccer ball and two goals for every seven players

Directions:

1. Place two goals approximately 30 yards apart.
2. Position players so that there are three offensive players in the middle of the field ready to score against two defenders.
3. Position two defenders at each end of the field.
4. On the coach's signal, the three offensive players pass the ball until they get close enough to the goal to shoot.
5. The player who takes the shot then joins the two defenders to try to score against the two defenders at the opposite end of the field.
6. If a defender steals a pass, that defending group goes on the attack with the person from whom they stole the pass.

Points to Emphasize: There is a numbers advantage for the offensive players so there should always be an open player. Encourage players to make switching and overlapping runs to create space. Challenge players by allowing them no more than two touches on the ball.

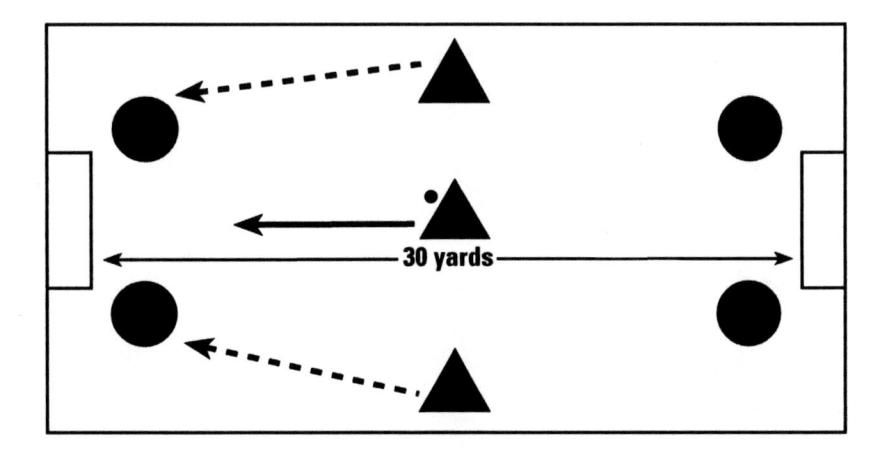

Drill #32: One-Versus-One Drill

Objective: To help develop decision-making abilities concerning passing choices with game-like defensive pressure.

Equipment Required: One soccer ball, one jersey for defender, two jerseys (different color from the defender's jersey) for neutral players, and four game markers for every four players

Directions:

Level 1
1. Position four players in a 15-yard-by-15-yard grid – one offensive, one defensive, and two neutral players.
2. The offensive player passes to one of the neutral players and then moves to open space to receive a return pass.
3. Players try to connect as many consecutive passes as possible.
4. If the defender gains possession, he becomes the offensive player.
5. After one minute of possession, switch roles.

Level 2
1. Use only one neutral player.
2. Apply a two-touch limit.

Points to Emphasize: Players must quickly change speeds and directions to create the spaces for passes. Variations of this drill include adding players to make two-versus-two or three-versus-three. Add goals to encourage finishing skills. Neutral players may not be defended.

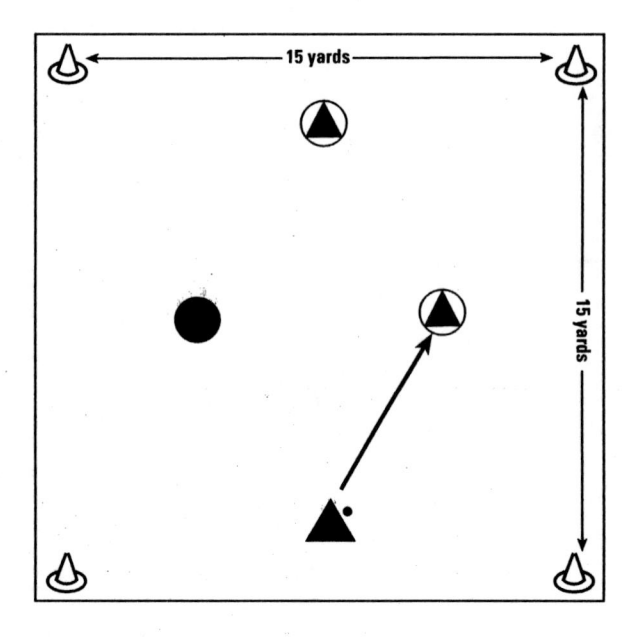

Drill #33: Partner Stationary Shooting Drill

Objective: To help develop proper kicking techniques for shooting a stationary ball from a stationary position with no defensive pressure.

Equipment Required: One soccer ball for every two players

Directions:

1. In a scattered formation, position partners so that they are 10 to 15 yards apart.
2. The partner without the ball should assume a goalkeeper's stance, with hands in a ready position.
3. The other partner will approach the stationary ball and shoot, trying to hit his partner.

Points to Emphasize: Beginning players are sometimes not accurate while shooting. To allow for this, it may be necessary to increase the number of goalkeepers a player is shooting toward. For example, space three goalkeepers in ready positions about 10 feet apart and have the shooter aim for the middle one. Players will spend less time chasing errant kicks. Reinforce a philosophy of accuracy over power during this drill. To help improve accuracy, encourage players to watch their foot strike the ball. Emphasize the use of the instep position of the foot as opposed to the toes.

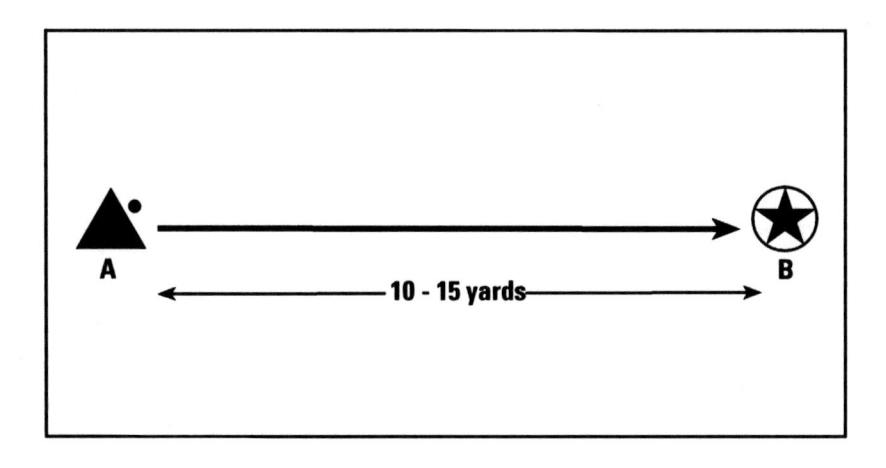

Drill #34: Three-Player Shooting Drill

Objective: To help develop proper kicking techniques for shooting a stationary ball from a stationary position with no defensive pressure.

Equipment Required: One soccer ball for every three players

Directions:

1. Position three players in a line approximately 10 yards apart.
2. Player A shoots the ball at player B, who is in a goalkeeper's stance.
3. Player B collects the ball and rolls it to player C.
4. Player C stops the ball and then shoots at player B.
5. After several shots, rotate players.

Points to Emphasize: Emphasize striking a stationary ball with the instep of the foot. Promote the philosophy of shooting accuracy over shooting power. As the players become more competent with shooting skills, increase the distance between players.

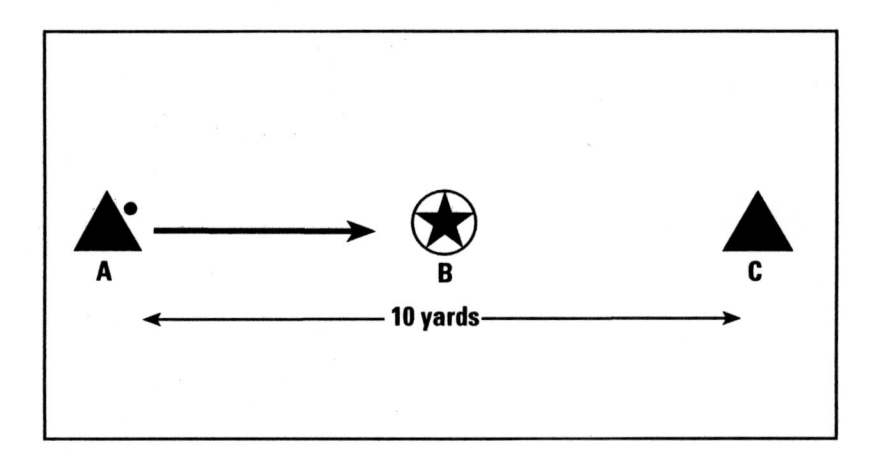

Drill #35: Open-Corner Drill

Objective: To help develop shooting accuracy from a stationary position with a stationary ball and no defensive pressure.

Equipment Required: One soccer ball per player, four goals

Directions:

Level 1
1. Place several balls in a row approximately 12 to 15 yards from the goal.
2. Players will shoot the balls into the unoccupied goal.

Level 2
1. Repeat Level 1 procedures 1 and 2.
2. Place a goalkeeper slightly to one side of the goal.
3. Challenge the players to shoot to the unoccupied corner.

Points to Emphasize: Once players have developed a proper kicking technique, they should develop an understanding of placement. Encourage players, during Level 1 of this drill, to shoot for the corners. When you add a goalkeeper at Level 2, restrict the keeper's movement by using game markers to establish how far he may move on the goal line. Do this drill as part of small-group work using portable or temporary goals, or as part of station work as players are arriving to practice. Using the drill in large-group work will result in too much standing.

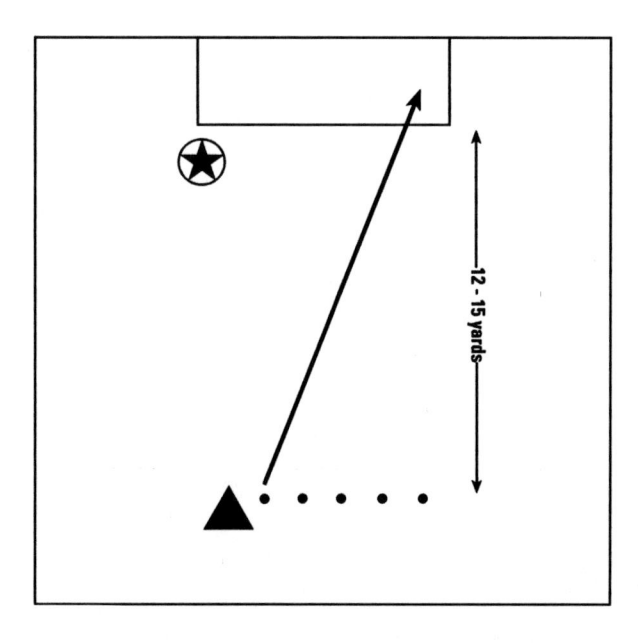

Drill #36: Run-and-Shoot Drill

Objective: To help develop proper kicking technique when the shooter is in motion, the ball is stationary, and there is no defensive pressure.

Equipment Required: Four soccer balls, one goal, four game markers for every four players

Directions:

Level 1
1. Place several balls in a row in a 15-yard-by-15-yard grid.
2. The shooter runs around one of the markers and shoots the ball in the goal.
3. Repeat several times with the shooter running around a different marker each time.

Level 2
1. Repeat Level 1 procedures 1 and 2.
2. Place a goalkeeper outside each goal post.
3. As the shooter makes the turn around the marker, signal one of the goalkeepers to step in one corner of the goal.
4. The shooter must shoot to the unoccupied corner.

Points to Emphasize: Requiring the shooter to run around different markers will vary the angle of the kick. During Level 2 action, goalkeepers must stay inside the goal on their side. This means shooters must look up to determine where to place the ball. During Level 1, one player shoots, two retrieve balls, and one player resets balls for next shooter. During Level 2, one player shoots, two act as goalkeepers, and the other retrieves balls. Coaches may want to use this drill as a station for circuit training. If you use this drill as a large-group activity, use regular and temporary goals. Emphasize shooting low at the temporary goals and high at the regular goals.

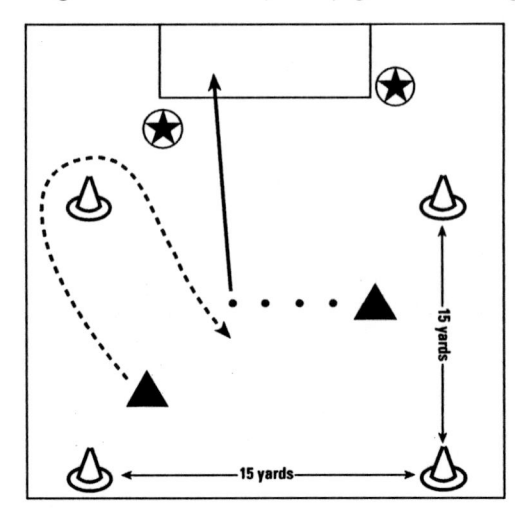

Drill #37: Pass-and-Shoot Drill

Objective: To help develop proper kicking technique by a stationary player shooting a moving ball with no defensive pressure.

Equipment Required: One soccer ball and two goals for every four players

Directions:

1. Place two goals 30 yards apart.
2. Position players as shown.
3. Player B serves to player C, who shoots at goalkeeper D.
4. Goalkeeper D passes to player C. Player C passes to player B, who shoots at goalkeeper A.
5. Repeat several times and reverse roles.

Points to Emphasize: Keep several balls in the goals for goalkeepers to pass. This keeps the drill fast paced. Encourage one-touch shooting to the corners of the goals.

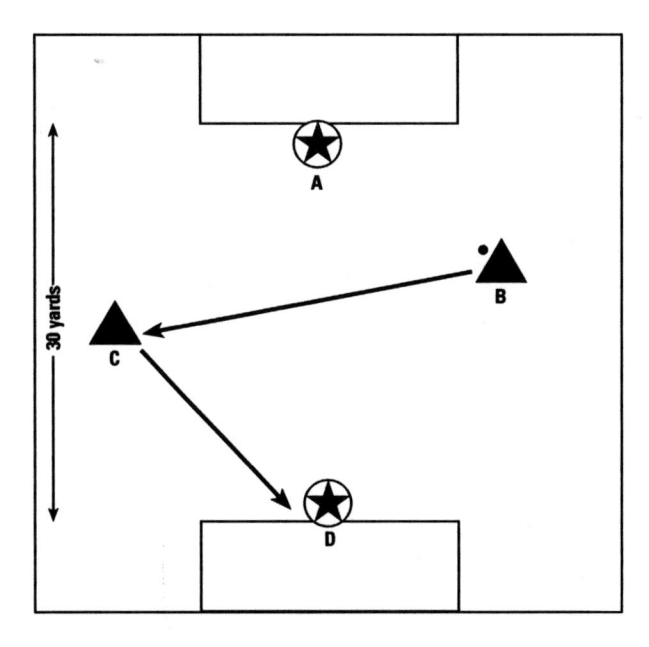

Drill #38: Over-the-Goal Shooting Drill

Objective: To help develop proper kicking technique for shooting a moving ball at various levels by a stationary player with no defensive pressure.

Equipment Required: Three soccer balls and one goal for every three players

Directions:

1. Position three players by placing one behind, one in front, and one in the goal.
2. Player A serves the ball over the goal to player C, who is approximately 15 to 20 yards from goal.
3. Player C shoots at goalkeeper B.
4. Player A will serve three balls; then players change roles.

Points to Emphasize: Moving balls served at various levels are very challenging for beginning players. Allow the shooter at least one touch to settle the ball a little before shooting. As skills improve, request that the players shoot the ball toward the goal on the first touch. Emphasize striking the middle or top half of the ball on its descent. This will help to keep the shot low.

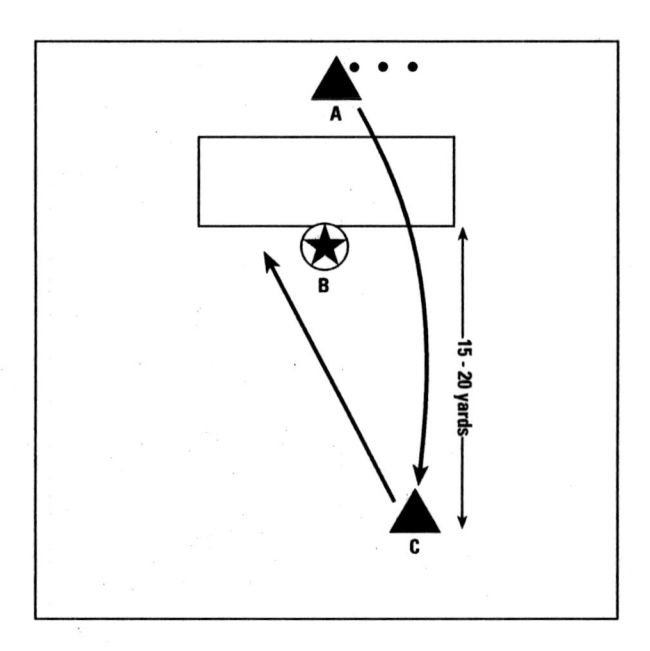

Drill #39: Alternating Shooting Drill

Objective: To help develop proper kicking technique for shooting a moving ball by a moving player with no defensive pressure.

Equipment Required: Four soccer balls and one set of goals for every four players

Directions:

1. Place two goals 30 yards apart.
2. Position two players in the center of the field.
3. Player B will serve balls alternately right and left.
4. Player A must go after the ball and shoot at the goal that is in the direction the ball is traveling.
5. Player A then returns to shoot in the opposite direction.

Points to Emphasize: Moving players shooting moving balls must gather a lot of information in a short time. They must compute the direction, speed, and level of the ball; their speed; their angle to the ball; their level relative to the ball; the distance from the goal; and the position of the goalkeeper. This is why the moving-ball-moving-player phase should be last in the shooting progression.

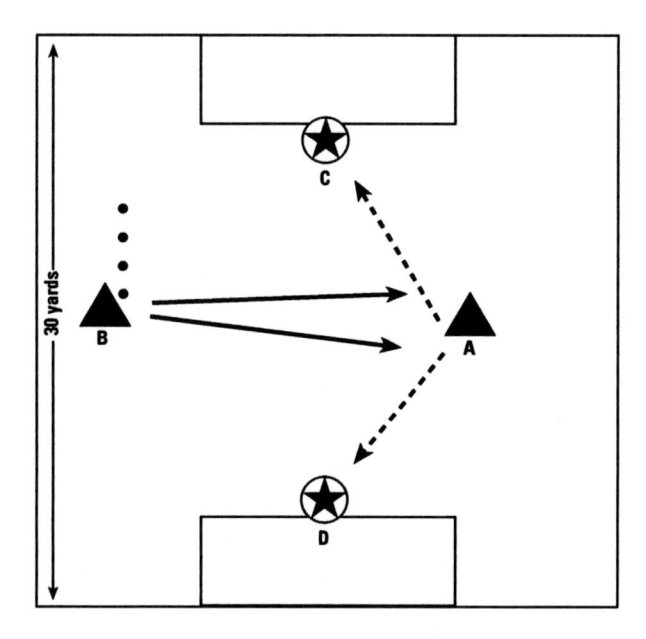

Drill #40: Spin-Turn Shooting Drill

Objective: To help develop creating space for shooting a moving ball by a moving player with no defensive pressure.

Equipment Required: One soccer ball and one goal for every two players

Directions:

1. Position players in the offensive third of the field.
2. Player A, in the penalty box, makes a horizontal run and then checks back for the ball.
3. Player B will pass to player A, who returns the ball to player B with a one-touch pass.
4. After returning the pass, player A spins to the outside to create space for player B to return pass for a shot.

Points to Emphasize: Players should pivot on the inside foot (the foot closest to the goal) when spinning to the outside. Players should alternate between spinning wide, to create enough space for a pass, and spinning close to the defender to get behind him.

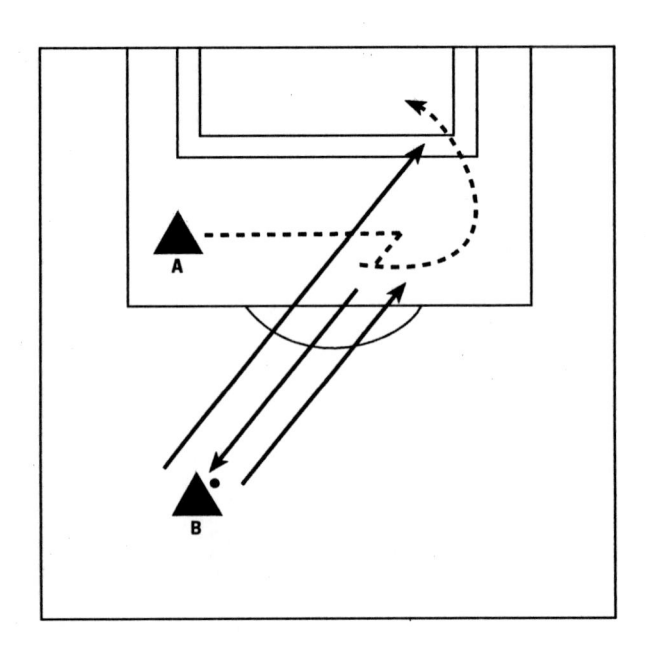

Drill #41: Circle-Pin Drill

Objective: To help develop shooting accuracy with subtle defensive pressure.

Equipment Required: One soccer ball, four game markers, one bowling pin for every six players

Directions:

1. Position five players to form a circle.
2. Inside the circle, place four game markers to form a square.
3. Place a bowling pin inside the square.
4. Designate a sixth player to defend the pin without going inside the square.
5. Players will pass the ball until a good shot opportunity is available.
6. If a player shoots and knocks down the pin, he replaces the defender.

Points to Emphasize: Emphasize to players that they should pass the ball quickly to make the defender change directions, thus creating space for a good shot.

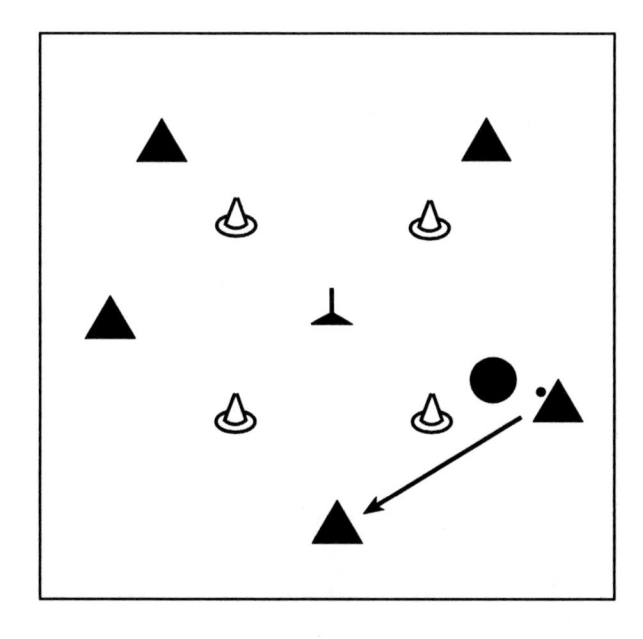

Drill #42: Three-Versus-One Shooting Drill

Objective: To help develop proper kicking techniques for shooting a moving ball by a moving player with subtle defensive pressure.

Equipment Required: One soccer ball and one goal for every four players, one jersey for every goalkeeper

Directions:

Level 1
1. Position players approximately 30 yards from the goal.
2. Offensive players A, B, and C connect a series of passes until one of them takes a shot.
3. One defender provides subtle pressure.

Level 2
1. Repeat Level 1 procedures 1 and 2.
2. Add a goalkeeper to provide more defensive pressure.

Points to Emphasize: Each offensive player must touch the ball before a shot may be taken. Encourage creative movement like switching and overlapping runs. To encourage goal scoring, give the offensive players a numbers advantage such as this drill provides.

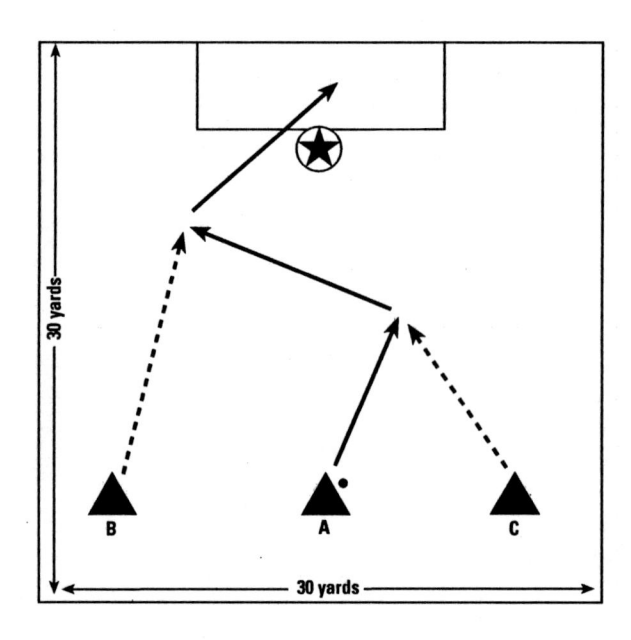

Drill #43: Wall Pass Shooting Drill

Objective: To help develop abilities to create space for shooting with game-like defensive pressure.

Equipment Required: One soccer ball and one goal for every four players

Directions:

Level 1
1. Position players in the defensive third of the field.
2. Player A is the offensive player; player B is the defender.
3. Player A must pass to player 1 or player 2, as a target, then move to open space for a return pass and shot.
4. Player B should defend aggressively.

Level 2
1. The ball is served to player A.
2. Player A must collect and take on the defender with individual moves to create space for a shot or use players 1 and 2 for wall passes.

Level 3
1. Repeat Level 2 procedures 1 and 2.
2. Add a goalkeeper to increase defensive pressure.

Points to Emphasize: Encourage players to change speeds, using quick bursts to create spaces for shots.

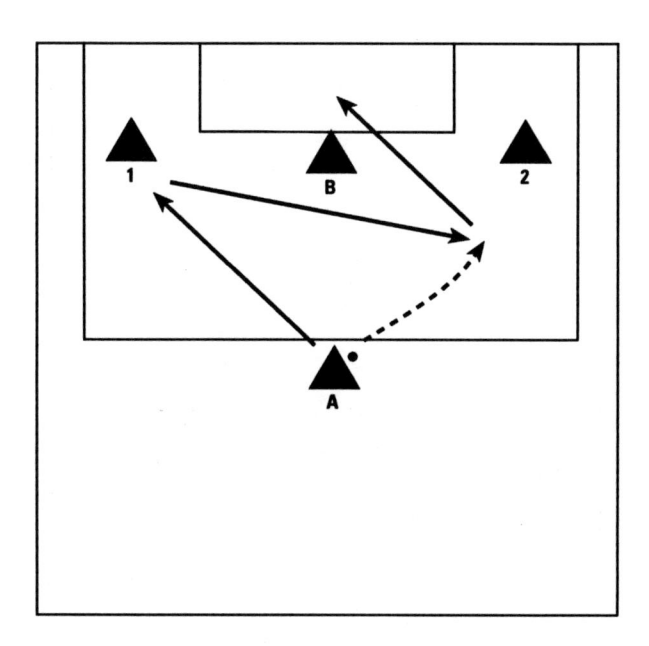

Drill #44: Line Drill

Objective: To help develop passing accuracy and collection skills from a moving player to a stationary target with no defensive pressure.

Equipment Required: One soccer ball and two game markers for every three players

Directions:

1. Place two game markers three to four yards apart.
2. Position three players in a line.
3. Player B passes to player A, who collects, dribbles toward player C, and passes to player C.
4. Player C collects and dribbles toward player B, who took the place of player A.
5. Repeat this action several times.

Points to Emphasize: This is a fast-paced drill that will provide lots of touches on the ball. Encourage players to make collection as easy as possible by delivering flat, soft passes.

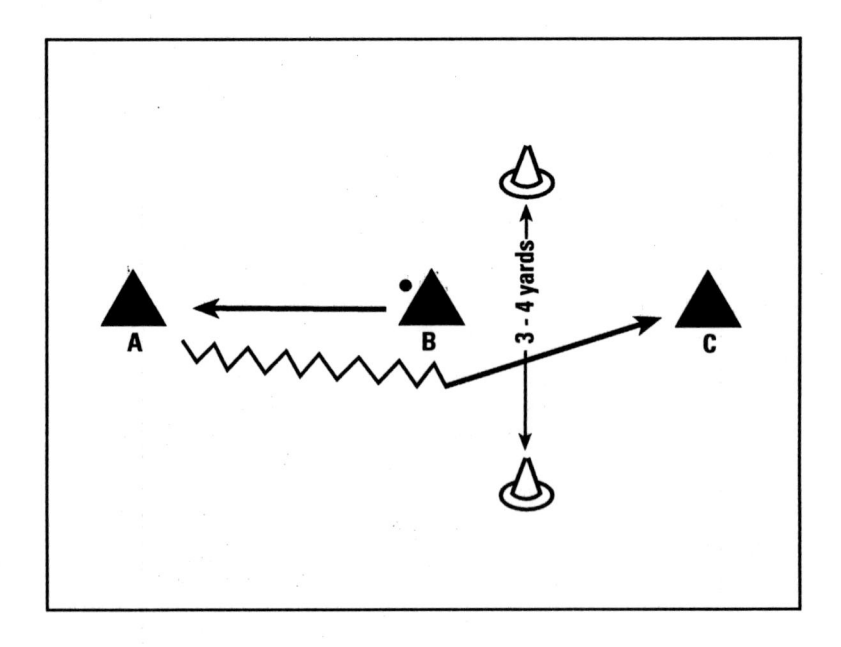

Drill #45: Pendulum Drill

Objective: To help develop passing accuracy and collection skills from a stationary passer to a moving target with no defensive pressure.

Equipment Required: Two soccer balls and four game markers for every three players

Directions:

1. Position three players in a 10-yard-by-10-yard grid.
2. Two players will each have a ball on one side of the grid.
3. A third player will be on the opposite side.
4. The player without the ball will move to the unoccupied corner.
5. As he moves, the player on that side will pass the ball.
6. The moving player will collect the ball and return it to the player who passed it to him, and then run to the corner he just left to receive a pass from the other player.
7. Continue this back-and-forth movement.
8. After one minute, switch roles.
9. After skills improve, play the pendulum game by counting how many passes a player can make in one minute.

Points to Emphasize: Encourage players to make flat passes with the correct amount of force that will be easy to collect. Discuss how the speed of the player will affect how far the passer must lead the pass.

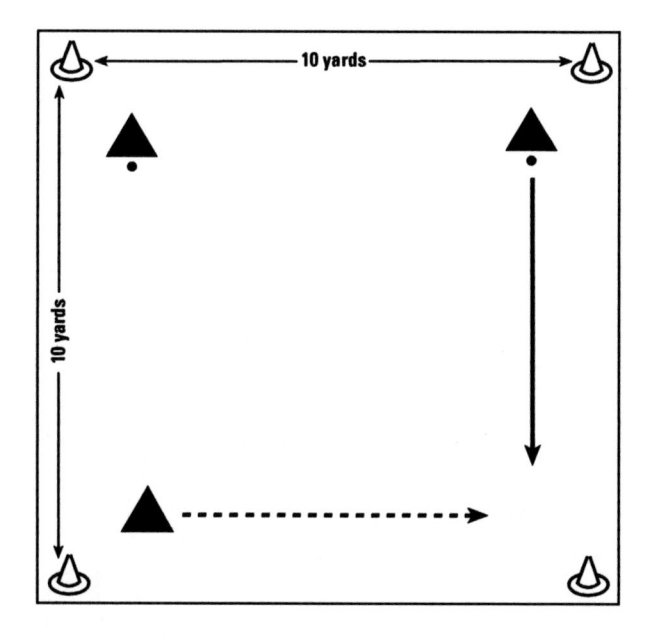

Drill #46: Invisible Man Drill

Objective: To help develop passing and collection skills with subtle defensive pressure.

Equipment Required: One soccer ball and four game markers for every three players

Directions:

1. Position three players in a 10-yard-by-10-yard grid.
2. Players should be in a straight line with players B and C looking in the direction of player A.
3. Player B can move laterally, but not forward or backward.
4. Player C moves either right or left to receive a pass from player A.
5. Player B then faces player C, and players repeat the action.
6. After several chances, change defenders.

Points to Emphasize: The addition of the defender will add a subtle pressure to the passer because it will affect his vision. In fact, if player C does not move into open space, he is practically invisible to player A.

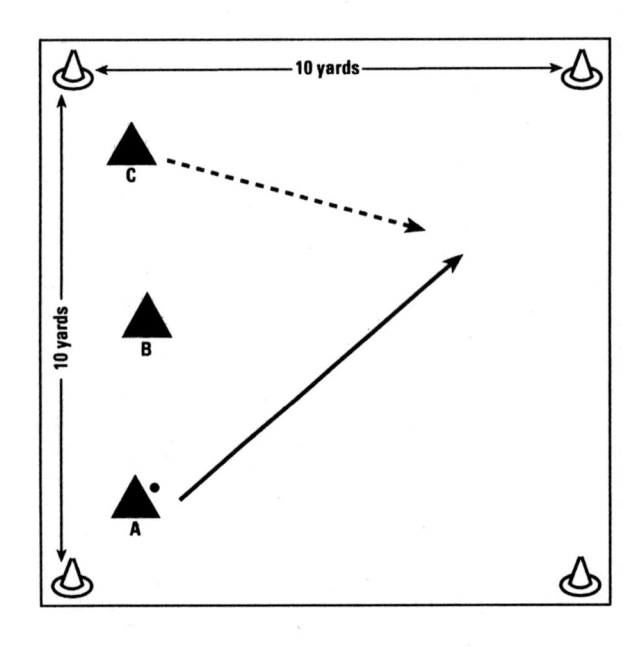

Drill #47: Beat-the-Clock Drill

Objective: To help develop passing and collecting skills with game-like defensive pressure.

Equipment Required: One soccer ball for every two players, four game markers, two sets of jerseys (one jersey for each player)

Directions:

1. Divide the group into two equal teams with different jerseys.
2. Position team A players, each with a ball, in a 30-yard-by-30-yard grid.
3. Members of team B are outside the grid.
4. On the coach's signal, players on team B enter the grid, they go to a support position so that teammates can pass them a ball.
5. After a team A player has his ball kicked out of the grid, he goes to a support position so that a teammate can pass him a ball.
6. The coach times how long it takes the defensive team to get all the balls out of the grid.
7. Then the teams switch roles.

Points to Emphasize: Team A players should move to open space to maintain possession of the ball. Should they lose possession, they should move to a support position where they will try to collect, look, and make a good decision as to where to play the ball next.

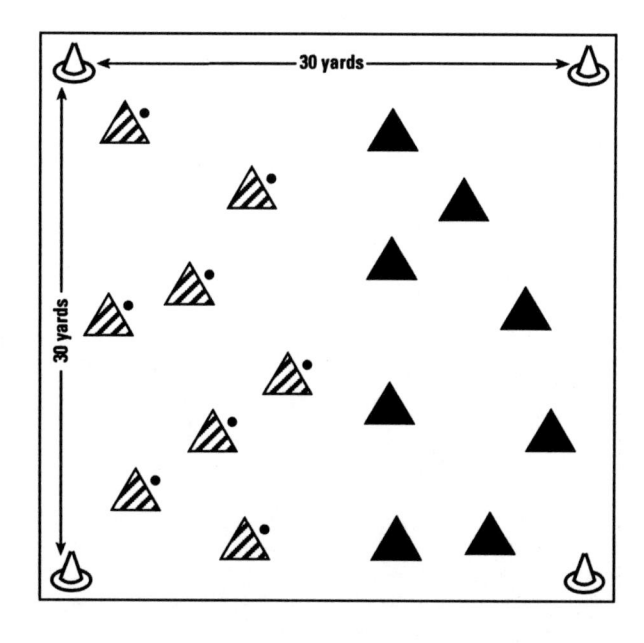

Drill #48: Toss-to-Self Heading Drill

Objective: To help develop the skill of striking the ball with the part of the forehead known as the hairline, with no defensive pressure.

Equipment Required: One foam or beach ball for every player

Directions:

Level 1
1. Position players in a scattered formation.
2. Players should be on their knees, each with a ball. Players toss the ball slightly above their heads, strike it gently with their heads, and then catch the ball before it strikes the ground.
3. Repeat several times.

Level 2
1. After players have demonstrated correct heading techniques, have them repeat this action from a standing position.

Points to Emphasize: Visually demonstrate to players the location of the hairline. Emphasize moving the head to strike the ball instead of merely positioning the head so the ball will hit it. Insist that players strike the ball with their eyes open and mouths closed. This will prevent them from biting their tongues later when using a harder ball. At Level 2 encourage players to establish a good base of support by slightly flexing their knees and positioning their feet a little more than shoulder-width apart.

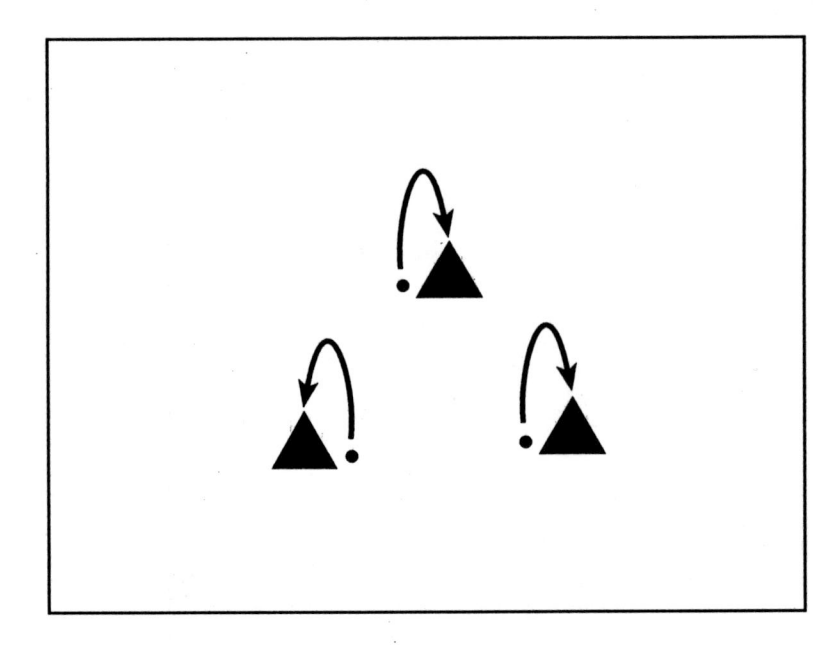

Drill #49: Partner Heading Drill

Objective: To help develop proper heading technique with no defensive pressure.

Equipment Required: One foam, sponge, or beach ball for every two players, four game markers

Directions:

Level 1
1. Position players in a 30-yard-by-30-yard grid with a partner.
2. Each set of players has a ball.
3. The player with the ball tosses to himself and heads the ball to his partner, who will catch, toss, and head it back.

Level 2
1. Instead of tossing to himself, the player tosses to his partner, who returns the ball by heading.
2. Players should be about five yards apart to begin this phase.
3. Gradually increase distance as both tossing and heading skills improve.

Level 3
1. The partner tosses to the player in motion, who returns the ball by heading.
2. The player in motion should vary directions forward, backward, left, and right.

Points to Emphasize: Partners should select a type of ball with which they feel comfortable. Emphasize bending at the waist in a backward direction and then thrusting forward to contact the ball to generate more force. Players should flex knees and extend arms to improve balance.

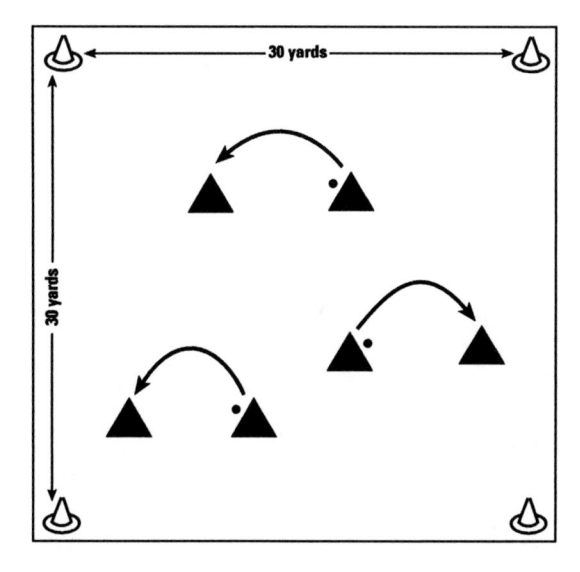

Drill #50: Short and Long Heading Drill

Objective: To help develop force relationships when heading with no defensive pressure.

Equipment Required: Two soccer balls and four game markers for every three players

Directions:

Level 1
1. Position three players in a 10-yard-by-10-yard grid.
2. Players B and C each have a ball.
3. Player B takes a position five yards from player A. Player B tosses to player A, who returns the ball by heading. Player C, who takes a position 10 yards from player A, then tosses, and player A repeats the heading action.

Level 2
1. After the first toss, only heading skills are allowed.
2. Player B tosses to player A.
3. Player A heads to player C.
4. Player C heads to player A, who returns the ball by heading to player B.
5. Repeat this action.

Points to Emphasize: Players will need to generate different amounts of force because of the varying distances the ball must travel. Emphasize that the speed with which the head strikes the ball is the major factor in generating this force. Players can increase head speed by bending at the waist and thrusting the upper body forward. At Level 2, use only one ball. Encourage players to move their feet to get good position for striking the ball.

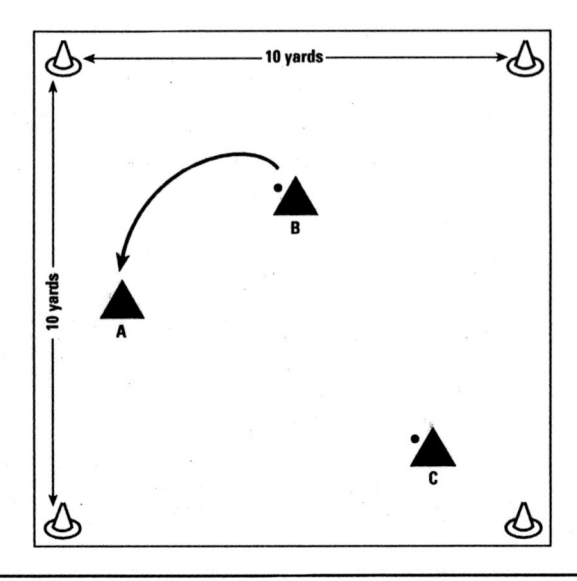

AFTERWORD

After reading this book, I hope you have a better understanding of what soccer is all about, the pitfalls that lie ahead, and how to avoid them whether you are a first-time coach, veteran coach, a player, or even a parent. I also hope that you don't think I am the most wonderful coach in the world, have all the answers, and never make mistakes. Hey, I've been fired more times than Billy Martin and Gaylord Perry, but each time I took away a positive experience. I've learned that it's not the getting fired, it's the getting hired that really counts. But, I think the most important thing I have learned in my 30-plus years of coaching kids, is that if I am true to my values, morals, and well-being, everything will fall into place. Sometimes it may look as if everything you're doing is wrong, but if you can be flexible and hang in there, all will be okay.

Never lie to kids! They can see through a phony better than anyone. If you lie to them one time, they will never trust you again. Always remember that soccer is fun. Most of the parents will not have a clue about what you are trying to do, although they might think they do. So, if you keep it fun, the kids – the most important people – will have a good time, learn a few things, and have some great memories – and so will you. I coached a girl from 8 to 12 years of age who said to me at her high school graduation, "Coach Thompson, I just wanted you to know that even though you were a hard coach and made us do drills and run and stuff, I never learned more or had more fun than when I played for you." This girl went on to Harvard and played soccer till she was about 21 years old. They ran out of math classes for her at Harvard. Someday she will find a cure for cancer or AIDs; I'm sure of it. That's the kind of stuff we coaches live for. All the other stuff, as today's youths would say, is ... OKAY.

I was once asked by a reporter, "What do you want your players to say about you after they have moved on." After thinking about it, I answered, "I hope they will take with them a love for competition. I hope they will feel I was fair. I know they will think I was tough, demanding, and sometimes hard on them, but I hope they will understand that it was all in the search for excellence within their own ability. But, the most important thing I would want them to say is that they had FUN!"

Fun is what coaching kids is all about. We coach soccer. But, it doesn't matter if it's soccer, basketball, softball, hockey, track, swimming, or field hockey. The one common thread should be that we as coaches must make it fun. Today's athletes are faster, stronger, and in better condition than we ever were. They are smarter, and they have more options than we ever dreamed of. In fact, today, if they can dream it, it will probably happen in their lifetime. They are more knowledgeable about conditioning, diet, and training, and as a group, they have a greater understanding of tactical play. However, there is also a lack of knowledge in today's athletes and that is where we as coaches can make a difference. The history of the game is being lost through the minutia of the skills and drills our players perform. We must teach them the history of the game, as well as the skills they need to succeed. They need to know how and why they are allowed to play in such outstanding facilities, and where the sport has been as well as where it may be going. If they are young boys, they need to hear about past pioneers, such as Kyle Rote, Jr., Ty Keogh, as well as Pelé. If they are young girls, they need to know about the struggles the women players have had to be recognized as athletes, the victories that have been won, Title IX, and why the names of Mia Hamm, Kristine Lilly, and Michelle Akers mean so much.

In Webster's dictionary, fun is defined as lively, joyous play for amusement sport or recreation, enjoyment or pleasure. Fun? Fun is playing soccer, learning new and exciting drills, techniques, skills every day, meeting new friends, and seeing old acquaintances. Fun is scoring a goal or making a great defensive play. Fun is watching your 9-year-old daughter catch the ball as a keeper and cheering for your 13-year-old son as he makes a great save as sweeper. Fun is showing up at practice early to work on corner kicks, staying late with the coach to work on a new drill, hanging out with all the boys or girls before a tournament game, and playing Marco Polo in the pool and elevator tag in the hotel. Fun is hearing your name called as they place the gold medal around your neck and playing beach soccer with friends just because you like the game. Fun is tournaments and more tournaments, collecting patches from other teams' players, and making the finals, as you finally realize what bonus points mean. Fun is hitting the ball just right with your laces, then looking at the crowd to see the happy faces. Fun is juggling a ball 10 times in a row, and heading the ball (when it doesn't hurt). Fun is making a run the full length of the field for the very first time, and making a move you've learned and having it work. Fun for a coach can be as simple as the look on a player's face when they first get to play, and the hugs of thanks at the end of the day. It's watching your daughter as she grows, learns, and develops new skills, and seeing your son play in a mud puddle in the rain. It's wins, losses, and the occasional tie. It's games in the rain, and under a clear blue sky. It's watching a 9-year-old player try a new move, and helping him reach way down, deep inside. It's the smiles and the tears, the anxiety and fears, and then when your day is done, it's time to pick up your bag and go home.

ABOUT THE AUTHOR

Howie Thompson is the head soccer coach at Southern High School in Durham, NC. Previously, he coached for 20 years in Connecticut at several high schools and started the Weston Girls Soccer Program in Weston, Connecticut. He has authored seven poems published by NSCAA magazine. He is the 2001 Five County High School Coach of the Year for Boys and the 2001 NSCAA Regional Coach of the Year for Girls Youth South Region.

The motto of Howie's coaching career has been threefold: to help kids, to help kids have fun, and to have fun helping kids. Howie says, "Soccer is a wonderful opportunity for the millions of children who are playing this great game all over our country. I hope that as soccer coaches and parents we can take a lesson from the baseball, hockey, and football parents who behave like the kids, and just enjoy the game for what it is. It's a game."

In his book, *Coaching Youth Soccer: A Complete Guide for Coaches, Players, and Parents*, Coach Thompson shares from his heart his experiences and lessons learned. He offers advice to coaches, parents, and players; outlines 50 of his favorite drills; and shares his humor and his poems.

The fun part of being a coach – postgame team pictures

00297 6630